Indoctrination, Education and God

For Carrie, with best love

Indoctrination, Education and God

The Struggle for the Mind

Terence Copley

First published in Great Britain in 2005

Society for Promoting Christian Knowledge
36 Causton Street
London SW1P 4ST

British Library Cataloguing-in-Publication Data

A catalogue record for this book is available from the British Library

ISBN 0-281-05682-X

1 3 5 7 9 10 8 6 4 2

Typeset by Avocet Typeset, Chilton, Aylesbury, Bucks
Printed in Great Britain by Ashford Colour Press

Contents

Acknowledgements   vi

Preface   vii

Introduction   xi

1 'Say What You Mean': The Meaning of Indoctrination,
   Secularization and Education   1
2 The Choking Cradle?: Religion Under Threat in English
   Society   21
3 'I've Got a Dog Now': The Death and Life of
   Christianity after 1945   45
4 Spiritual Fruits, not Religious Nuts: Replacing 'Religion'
   with 'Spirituality'   83
5 Education or Catastrophe?   105
6 Fighting a Vapour?: Secularization, Religion, Education
   and the Future   135

References   151

Bibliography and Further Reading   161

Index   169

Acknowledgements

Real thanks are due to various people and organizations that helped in the writing of this book. Alan Rusbridger, editor of the *Guardian*, wrote to answer my queries about newspaper reporting policy for religious news. The Catholic Education Service provided the figures listed on p. 80. Claire Copley had conducted postgraduate research into religion in English society and particularly into 'Christianity on campus', including the role of student religious societies. She allowed me access to findings discussed on p. 76ff. Rob Freathy is an expert on the history of citizenship in the UK curriculum and the thoughts on p. 117f. are informed by conversations with him. Huw Tudur is a Key Stage 2 teacher at Ysgol Santes Tudful, Merthyr Tudful, and 2004 President of Undeb Cenedlaethol Athrawon Cymru (UCAC), the Welsh Teachers' Union. He provided me with English translations of parts of his presidential address to Conference 2004 about national identity and memory. The University of Exeter granted me study leave in the Lent Term 2004. Virve Valtanen provided the reference for Catherine Booth on p. 86. The Reverend John Williams, General Secretary of the Wesleyan Reform Union, allowed me to test my theories about the survival of that denomination on him, adding ideas of his own and providing information about the denomination's recent history.

Preface

This book is about indoctrination and education. We will arrive at what these two have done to God later. But it is not about indoctrination as we usually think of it, religious indoctrination, in such matters as the rather tired debate about whether faith schools are divisive or whether they are indoctrinating children into religious belief. Our concern is the opposite. It is whether a secular indoctrination process is at work in British and European society, programming people against religious belief and, if so, whether education is an accomplice in this. Why is it that we are on constant alert against religious indoctrination while at the same time almost completely unprepared for secular indoctrination? Religious discourse and options in favour of belief have been effectively closed down or edited out for many people. People in Britain are frequently negative, even hostile, towards institutional Christianity, while at the same time being less critical of 'other religions' (except perhaps Islam), even more uncritical towards alternative spiritualities and, finally, completely uncritical of secular values. Four different levels of criticism, from near hostility to the suspension of disbelief, are being applied.

Are our children being inducted into this quadruple set of standards? I observed the attitudes and assumptions of children every working day during 15 years as a schoolteacher. If we want to assess what is happening in British society in terms of indoctrination, we have to include education in the equation. Education is the only universal activity in British society, along with shopping and watching television. Education occupies at least 11 full-time years – for many people, with nursery and university, 16 years. Translated into other terms, the 11 years minimum represents 440 weeks excluding holidays, or 2,200 days, or 12,100 teaching hours (minimum), or more than 7 per cent of a female lifetime. This excludes all post-16 education. The only rival in terms of hours spent in the life of most children is television and, for fewer, the internet. How does education shape hearts and minds during these 12,100-minimum hours? At present I lead research into religious education and train RE teach-

ers on the Postgraduate Certificate in Education (PGCE) programme. This takes me into many classrooms and many types of
school. If university work constitutes the proverbial 'ivory tower', it
is worth noting that you can view a wide territory from a tower, seeing things not always visible on the ground. In addition, for many
years I have researched and taught Victorian theology as well. That
is germane to this book, as some of the roots of what is happening
now can be traced back to Victorian times, to industrialization and
the rise and fall of 'modernity'. Out of these professional experiences came the questions that prompted this book.

The collapse of the Sunday school movement (see p. 50) left most
British children with no contact point with institutional Christianity
at all. Yet, apart from a tiny minority schooled at home, every child
attends a place of education. It is a truism that not every child attends
a place of worship. So children get their impressions of churches,
mosques, synagogues, mandirs and gurdwaras and, more importantly, the beliefs and values of those who frequent them, from their
own family – if these matters are ever mentioned at home – or from
their school and from the media. What if the impressions they are
receiving are mis-impressions? What if young people are never in a
real position to choose between a religious way of life and a non-
religious way of life? What if they irresistibly acquire a non-religious worldview in the same way they acquire a taste for jeans, logo
trainers and pop music?

From the point of view of faith communities such as the churches,
the question of the struggle for the mind is more important than they
perhaps realize. The churches have had to deal with the social results
of the secularization process – falling numbers and increasing social
marginalization. One result has been the impetus given to the
inward-looking ecumenical movement with its quaint 'conversations' about doctrine and polity, its schemes and covenants and occasional mergers (e.g. the Methodists in 1932, the United Reformed
Church in 1972). None of these time-consuming activities has
demonstrably made the slightest difference to the drift away.
Alongside the time spent on this ecumenical industry, or perhaps
because of it, there has been a notable failure in Christian apologetic
to speak from the changed situation, other than the conservative re-
iteration of what was or the liberal dash to espouse every latest
trendy philosophical fad. A few religious commentators have

embraced secularization while others have deplored it. Not many have critiqued it. Not much of a struggle for the mind has actually occurred.

Can the churches take comfort from the fact that more than a quarter of the nation's children attend church primary schools? What if these too have witnessed a secularization of mind? A notice board outside a school stating that it is St Nemo's Church of England (VA) Primary School in itself provides no evidence that the religious or Christian option will be presented more than nominally behind the closed doors of the classroom. Current attacks by some on the existence of faith schools on the grounds that they are divisive or indoctrinatory by virtue of their very existence entirely miss the point. We have to know what is happening on the inside. Some people can testify fervently that having been to a faith school has put them off faith, rather than communicated a living faith to them. So faith schools require a more sophisticated level of debate. All schools reflect and transmit values, secular or religious. We should be examining the values of community schools as well, and looking for a different sort of indoctrination.

We also need to take account of the sincerity of the beliefs and spirituality of the many adults who have no contact with institutional religions. They are not in the main atheists, nor are they secularists, i.e. atheists who are striving to advance the secularization process and dethrone religion. They stand as a rather mute mass reminder that the secularization thesis does not explain beliefs away and that when Matthew Arnold, in his poem 'Dover Beach' (1867), spoke of the sea of faith retreating, this was not a good metaphor for his purpose. Tides turn, even in those places like Weston-super-Mare where they recede a very long way. Perhaps British Christianity has reached its Weston-super-Mare. Secularization is still advancing relentlessly, but more in England than the rest of the UK and more in the UK than Europe and much more in Europe than the planet. What role has the specific English and UK dimension – historical, cultural, social – played? Have British people lost touch with their cultural roots? Is it one of the last relics of Empire that the English mindset still assumes that England is typical of the UK and the world, or is even at its centre?

This book attempts to explore this complex and, as we shall see, sometimes contradictory situation. It asks whether a form of secular indoctrination is occurring and whether education, the media and specifically English or British factors might be complicit in this process. I am also keenly interested in whether what is referred to in shorthand as 'God' can be dispensed with quite so easily. For Christians, the resurrection should be a reminder that God can re-appear when God is definitely dead and buried. No wonder the disciples were tight-lipped and terrified (Mark 16.8).

Terence Copley
School of Education and Lifelong Learning
University of Exeter

Introduction

If we were being indoctrinated now, at this very minute, would we know? What if it were a rather pleasant or at least imperceptible experience, unlike the stereotypes of indoctrination in George Orwell's *Nineteen Eighty-Four* or the state machine in Nazi Germany or the techniques of North Korea? If such indoctrination were happening, would it be more likely to be religious indoctrination or secular indoctrination? In other words, are we more likely in today's society to be indoctrinated into religion, or out of it? If such indoctrination were secular, would it not be a supremely clever ploy to put people on their guard against religious indoctrination, which the British have been wary of for centuries, while all the time this other indoctrination was actively in progress? Of course, this is not just a British affair. In 2004 the US law firm Cadwalader, Wickersham & Taft took action in the Supreme Court against the American Pledge of Allegiance, 'one nation under God', on behalf of Buddhists who rejected God. But removing God from the Pledge is not value neutral. It simply tilts the balance towards agnosticism or atheism.

If a process of secular indoctrination is occurring, it might easily be perceived in apocalyptic terms by some religious believers, as the product of dark or demonic forces working to a concerted plan. Or it could be interpreted as an entirely impersonal process, which has just come about as a result of a complex of social and cultural factors from the Enlightenment to post-modernity, accelerating from Victorian times and again from the 1960s onwards. Such a process would not be effective unless it either neutralized or conquered the education system. But the education system itself is ripe for ideological or philosophical conquest. It has become a massive and unwieldy machine, from the cradle via nursery and pre-school provision, through the years of compulsory schooling (ages 5 to 16), through post-compulsory schooling, further education, higher education, in-service training and finally arriving at 'E3A', education for the 'third age'.

'Do you know who made you?'

'Nobody, as I knows on ... I 'spect I grow'd. Don't think nobody never made me.'

The UK education machine resembles Topsy in Harriet Beecher Stowe's *Uncle Tom's Cabin*. It can be shown to possess, rather than to be aware of, a parentage within the history of ideas, but for all practical purposes this has been forgotten.

It has escaped the attention of many commentators that as institutional religion has declined in Britain, institutional education has risen to greater and greater heights, 'widening participation', 'raising standards' and the extension of its wonderful benefits to two-year-olds being three recent mantras. In Wales this process can be seen at work in a specifically Welsh way. As the role of the chapels in preserving the Welsh language declined with their congregations, the preservation role was taken over by the Welsh education system and the position of the Welsh language in the Welsh national curriculum. Perhaps the UK education system is preserving religion, or the shell of religion, after the decline of the churches.

In some ways liberal education appears to function rather like a religion, offering rewards, self-esteem, happiness, to those willing to devote themselves to the disciplined path of study for GCSE or PhD or evening class. In more optimistic times education was seen as a part of the upward progress of humankind. Education was considered automatically beneficial. Can we speak in these terms after the dark epiphanies of Auschwitz and 9/11, and when post-modernity seems to leave us clinging to the fragments of our dismembered selves, adrift in a universe which seems תהו ובהו, 'formless and void' (Genesis 1.1)? We look on Aztec sacrificial blood-letting with disgust, but modern Europe has collectively indulged in blood-letting on a far larger scale in two world wars and numerous acts of 'ethnic cleansing', frequently using sacrificial language derived from religion. 'Education' did not prevent Auschwitz. It may even have fuelled the process by curriculum control, as did science and technology in streamlining the factory production lines of death. What are the aims of education now? Its values? Its underpinning beliefs? Whom is it serving? To whom is it accountable? The UK witnesses almost constant reorganization of some part of the education system, undertaken almost always with neither any discussion of what the whole enterprise is supposed to achieve nor adequate capital investment. Significantly, the study of the philosophy of education has dwindled, even in university departments of education. The last deep national debate about education took place in 1943 when bombs were falling on London.

It is also significant that while British society seems able to live with 'spirituality', however it may be conceived, 'religion' is perceived as a problem. At the very least it is an embarrassment, as any religious education teacher can testify. Revealing their occupation is a very good conversation stopper for RE teachers at parties. A London vicar remarked to me that when he walks down Oxford Street with his clerical collar on, the crowds of shoppers part like the waters of the Red Sea for him to pass. If it was ever the fashion to be religious, it must now be the fashion *not* to be religious. Put another way, religious adherence is one of the most 'uncool' social activities one could imagine, especially for the young. But has it ceased to be a real choice altogether? Would it even cross the mind of the hundreds of thousands, perhaps millions, of people out shopping on Sunday morning that they might go to a place of religious worship as well or instead? Curiously, the one group that has historically taken the Christian religion to the people, the Salvation Army, continues to do so clad in post-Victorian raiment but uncompromisingly wearing its original Victorian beliefs. The 'Sally Army' has become part of British cultural eccentricity and is much patronized, in both senses of the word, for its welfare work.

It is important to recognize that the notion of religion as a problem is emphatically not global. Across the surface of the planet religions are alive and well. They are extremely potent forces – not always for moral good – in the lives of women and men. Their meta-narratives or grand stories to account for the meaning of life and the universe influence billions, even if our island section of the planet has gone into a post-modern phase, which finds meta-narrative difficult. Religion is not uncool in El Salvador or South Korea or the USA or the Philippines or Syria or India or Zambia. There is no evidence to suggest that, taking the planet as a whole, religion is on the way out. So the UK and Europe, neither of them, significantly, the cradle of any major world religion, must have developed a particular problem or seen a particular light. As a classroom teacher for many years, I noticed that every day children make generalizations about religions based entirely on the British scene. The UK, or often England, is the world of their mindset, despite all that is written about the effect of global cultures and multinational corporations.

Yet despite what looks very much like the popular abandonment of institutional religion in Britain, individual religious beliefs persist. In what is variously labelled a rational, secular, plural, multicultural, post-Christian, post-modern society, 71.6 per cent of people in the UK according to the 2001 national census still express adherence to Christianity, with the other religions represented registering significant percentage points. What is going on? On what basis can we say these people are 'secular'? Commentators on religion are divided between qualified optimism about the future of religion (Grace Davie) and cheerful, almost gleeful, pessimism (Callum Brown). Some of the faithful bewail the willing participation of the churches in their own marginalization by restricting their work and teaching to an emphasis on Christian social welfare and an embracing of secular thought (Edward Norman). The call for a confident, authoritarian Church, urging people to repentance in the name of the man who was truly God and died to save them from their sins, is not restricted to Norman. Such churches seem to be surviving much better than their 'liberal' or 'social gospel' counterparts.

But many people are quite happy getting on with their lives minus institutional religion, without any particular consciousness of sin or guilt or that something is missing. Does the Church have to make them unhappy, guilty or inadequate before it can preach salvation and 'rescue' them from a life crisis it has immorally created? Is it really possible to herd everyone along that straight and narrow path? Collectively, UK churches present as unconfident, internally divided (e.g. about gay issues) and arcane (still resisting the equality of women). It is incomprehensible to outsiders that the largest UK church in terms of Sunday attendance, the Roman Catholic Church, still has no women priests and imposes celibacy upon its male priests. Small wonder to any external observer that if repressed in involuntary celibacy, the male sex drive will burst out in some other way, including child abuse as one deviant possibility. All this discredits the Church, making it look not only out of date but *unnatural* in the eyes of outsiders, before its central beliefs have even been thought about. This is not the scandal of Christ crucified (1 Corinthians 1.23) but the scandal of Christ's followers losing the plot. Other churches are by no means immune from this loss of direction.

Unlike the USA, where success breeds success and the churches often have modern, lavishly kept buildings and at least decent congregations numerically, the UK scene provides a picture not only of decline but of decay. In a situation when they lack confidence, have lost direction and are in a state of deterioration, the UK churches cannot be surprised if the clear and apparently simple message of Islam appeals to some UK citizens rather more than their unclear message. Converts say that they find in Islam all the things that 150 years ago converts said they found in Christianity. These include clear guidance on living; a sense of community or family; a sense of God at the centre of life; meaning and purpose for everyday living; an unequivocal moral code; authoritative scriptures to live by. These answers could apply to more than one religion. Is it any more than accident which religion converts 'find'? In any case, are those in search of authoritative answers any more than a minority?

What if the majority are being indoctrinated in such a way that they never see the question, let alone start assessing truth claims that provide possible answers? When I was in training as a teacher of RE, I was told that the great religions of the world have grown up to answer the questions that humankind perennially poses and which the children I was poised to teach would ask. In retrospect this was a very humanistic view of religions, which ignores the claims of revelation. Religions, after all, make truth claims to which we are challenged to respond – if we ever become aware of them. Now that I train RE teachers, I wonder whether the children my graduate students are preparing to teach are asking questions of meaning at all. Does it matter? Has something happened to remove their questions? They inhabit a more secular world, or, perhaps better expressed, it inhabits their minds.

Secularization has been extensively addressed by sociologists of religion. I wanted to see what is happening by taking a wider frame than simply sociology, to include also church history, theology, the history and philosophy of education, politics and study of the media. Whatever has happened and is happening, it is a process much wider than the orbit of institutional religion, yet much of the academic debate has focused on the position of the churches in a secularizing society. We cannot ignore the churches, but why not also examine what is happening to education in this process? Could it be that education has unwittingly become one key factor in the secularization of the British or European mind?

Then came a personal experience of my own, not on the Damascus road but in a supermarket. It is about five years now since hot cross buns, at one time a clear annual Christian symbol linked to Holy Week and Good Friday, went the way of chocolate eggs and began to appear all the year round in the supermarkets. This is a minor, but indicative, example of secularization. The religious symbol is separated from its story and so becomes meaningless. On Christmas Eve of the first year I noticed this, I picked up a packet and asked to see the supermarket manager. Obtaining an interview with some difficulty, I asked why these hot cross buns were on sale that day. Horrified, the manager snatched the packet and examined it with the words: 'What! Are they past their sell-by date?' This provides a very vivid reminder of how far the signals of Christianity have disappeared or been secularized, like the apocryphal story of a customer in a jeweller's shop, buying a cross, who is asked, 'Do you want a plain one, or one with a little man on?' The comedian Jasper Carrott retold this joke on TV in 2004. The fact that the studio audience laughed suggests that some religious literacy remains. To laugh they had to know who the little man was. But if the signals are disappearing, does it follow that a form of secular indoctrination is relentlessly advancing? Where should religious education position itself in this situation? Is RE the King Canute of curriculum, ineffectually bidding the tide of secularization turn back?

The influence of curriculum and its underlying values is similar to the long-debated question of the influence of television. Since TV adverts have a measurable influence in terms of product sales figures, we must presume the programmes have some influence too. The crudely measurable influence of the curriculum is seen in examinations and testing – but what is the subterranean influence? Radically understood, curriculum is really a dream on the part of its planners, about the world we inhabit and the world we wish to inhabit, and about children growing up into both worlds. Whether this dream is a vision or a nightmare depends on the values and beliefs of the planners and the values of the observer. But did the planners of British curriculum have a dream at all, or just a set of muddled assumptions? Although the story that the English and

Welsh national curriculum was conceived in 1988 on the back of an envelope in a train in a tunnel in London is almost certainly untrue, it appears plausible. Yet however muddled it might be, curriculum is still a powerful tool, by virtue of the 'subjects' or components it blesses with time and resources and those it places on the periphery or even starves. Those curriculum subjects that are taught on the perimeter of the secondary school campus in Portakabins long past their use-by date are bound to lose status. Do they also move to the perimeter of the child's mind? Where is the RE classroom situated?

The evidence with which we are concerned will largely be drawn from England. This is neither a claim nor an assumption of English superiority, but a constraint imposed by the length of the book. Much of what is found would apply equally to Scotland, Wales or the UK as a whole, perhaps to Europe and possibly to some other English-speaking countries as well. Is the apparent western distaste for or unease about religion connected with uncertainty about national identity? English and UK identities are both unclear and it is still uncertain to what extent the UK owns a European identity. What if the British have grown up in and now inhabit a religious desert island and are basing their generalizations entirely on that? The central issue we are seeking to explore is how far an implicitly secular indoctrination is occurring in society and, if so, whether education is helping or hindering this process. Is the steady flow of pessimism about 'religion' from the 1960s onwards likely to be reversed in a still young century? What forces are winning at present in the struggle for the mind? It is time to raise the curtain on the story.

1

'Say What You Mean': The Meaning of Indoctrination, Secularization and Education

'Then you should say what you mean,' the March Hare went on.
(Lewis Carroll, *Alice's Adventures in Wonderland*,
1865, Chapter 7)

Centuries do not begin at the stroke of midnight on 31 December in the year '99. Epochs and eras are marked by events. So the nineteenth century is commonly said by historians to have ended with the assassination of the Archduke Francis Ferdinand on 28 June 1914, leading to a Great War so encompassing that it changed subsequent world history and the way in which people thought. Its mute stone testimonies remain in every town and village, with their lists of the 'glorious dead', frequently inscribed with the brave hope that their names will live for evermore. Then, although it escaped the notice of most commentators at the time, the twentieth century ended on 11 September 2001 with the infamous events in New York and Washington DC. These were witnessed at the time or shortly afterwards by billions of people via the medium of television. The events of '9/11' will continue to fascinate and repel and to evoke analysis throughout the twenty-first century, rather as the sinking of the *Titanic* obsessed the twentieth. For what was done on 9/11 was done in the name of religion, even though right-minded believers in the religion in question continue to deny its title to a religious act. Islam was hijacked on that day as well as aeroplanes.

In a society variously labelled 'secular', 'plural', 'post-modern', it comes as a profound shock to many Europeans when religion is taken seriously, so seriously that people are prepared to die for it, or even to kill other human beings for it. This has not really happened in Europe on a large scale since the Thirty Years War ended in 1648. The events of 9/11 therefore reinforce the view of some people that we are better off without religion, as it has the potential to cause serious harm. It is then easier to affirm the common dictum that 'it doesn't matter what you believe, as long as you lead a good life'. For we have come to believe – yes, this too is a *belief* – that religion is itself an optional set of beliefs which one adopts or not, as a matter of personal choice. Religion is seen as a leisure pursuit. A private matter. A harmless, sometimes philanthropic, hobby. That is why 9/11 is so shocking. One would not die or kill for darts or golf or Scrabble or Oxfam. Or discuss religious beliefs at the office. We have continued in our schools to teach sanitized versions of religions, partly as a result of a proper, scrupulous concern not to indoctrinate children into religious belief. Rather less attention has been paid to whether this process might instead have indoctrinated them into a polite and respectful agnosticism, which is content to leave religions alone provided religions leave us alone.

Throughout this book we shall be fundamentally concerned with three inter-linking processes: indoctrination, secularization and education, and what they have each 'done' to God. Each of them has a vast literature stream and this is not the place to attempt to produce exhaustive summaries of what has been written in each field. Theology has produced its own version of secularization, in the writings of D. F. Strauss, Ludwig Feuerbach, Dietrich Bonhoeffer, Rudolph Bultmann, Paul van Buren, Don Cupitt and others. They have each sought in some way to demythologize Christianity and reduce it or translate it into its essentials, stated in secular language. What has resulted has often been inconsistent and always reductionist. But who can blame them for trying during two centuries which found 'orthodoxy' frequently unintelligible and increasingly difficult to reconcile with intellectual honesty? What makes this book different from the corpus of books in each of the three fields identified is that we shall be considering indoctrination, secularization and education in relation to each other and in relation to a specific context: religion in British, more often English, society.

Indoctrination

What is indoctrination? How does it operate? Doctrine is simply the defined tenets, usually of a sect or religion. So indoctrination in its neutral sense is just the teaching or inculcation of doctrine. Doctrine does not have to be conveyed by an individual. It could be transmitted by a group of people or by an impersonal process. By attending the services of a church on a weekly basis for a year or more, one might learn basic Christian doctrine, as a result of exposure to creeds, Bible readings, hymns, etc. W. H. Kilpatrick notes that in the *Oxford English Dictionary*, indoctrination was defined only in these non-pejorative terms as late as 1910. In the Second World War, the word was used by the US Navy to mean 'the fundamentals of military discipline, naval customs and usage'.[1] However, this usage has died out and in common with its sister word, propaganda, doctrine has acquired sinister connotations from these more innocent beginnings. It is associated with the questionable moral activity of instilling particular beliefs or values into the unwilling or the unaware. The dictionary still retains its less pejorative sense, hence, for example, the first meaning given in the *Dictionary of the English Language* (Longman, 1984):

> **1** to instruct, esp in fundamentals or rudiments; teach **2** to imbue with partisan or sectarian opinion, point of view or ideology [prob fr ME *endoctrinen* . . . en + doctrine].

Every culture and society inducts its young into its beliefs and values and provides them with a worldview – their unquestioning assumptions about life and values – of which they may remain unconscious throughout their life while at the same time being profoundly influenced, even moulded, by it. In that sense all societies can be said to indoctrinate their young. The 'doctrine' in that context is the view of the world taken for granted in the host culture. In this context, enculturization, conditioning and indoctrination are difficult to disentangle. H. Ziebertz speaks of the *Lebensweltlich*, the pre-conditioning of pupils before a learning process starts. He notes its derivation from *Lebenswelt*, the sub-conscious, pre-conditioned, socio-cultural way of viewing the world and life.[2]

I. A. Snook, writing from the standpoint of moral philosophy and the culture of New Zealand, argues that although content and methods are important aspects of indoctrination, intention is paramount. A doctrine in his view is a statement which 'cannot *in principle* [his italics] be shown to be either true or false'.[3] He links doctrine indissolubly with indoctrination: 'Only doctrines can be indoctrinated'.[4] Indoctrination is concerned with propositional knowledge, 'knowing *that . . .*'

A person indoctrinates P (a proposition or a set of propositions) if he teaches with the intention that the pupil or pupils believe P regardless of the evidence.[5]

Barrow and Woods see all political, religious and moral systems of belief as doctrinal.[6] Teaching an ideology as if it were the only one; teaching propositions as certain that the teacher knows to be uncertain or even false: these are indoctrinatory according to Snook. In contrast, teaching 'facts' (e.g. multiplication tables, Latin verbs) and teaching young children acceptable behaviour (e.g. not to eat peas from a knife) – are not indoctrination. He acknowledges grey areas: inculcating beliefs the teacher sincerely believes are certain but which are substantially disputed; teaching any subject without due concern for student understanding.[7]

Snook usefully distinguishes indoctrination from 'brainwashing', even though in casual conversation the two are sometimes used interchangeably. Brainwashing uses 'all known methods to change a person's pattern of thinking and feeling: conditioning, anxiety, fear, indoctrination, distortions, drugs, group analyses, enforced isolation.[8] Another distinction from brainwashing is provided by John Wilson. He argues that 'it is peculiar to indoctrination that the will of the person is not over-ridden'.[9] Those who have been indoctrinated into particular beliefs *mean* them; those who have been conditioned or brainwashed into them cannot be said to hold them with meaning.[10] Indoctrination leads someone to believe something that is irrational.[11] For Ben Spiecker indoctrination aims to 'suppress wilfully [the development of] the critical disposition of the students'.[12] Jürgen Oelkers says that education becomes indoctrination when it has the power to fix habits or dispositions without the participation of the child's active powers.[13] John Hull suggests that the indoctrinator disguises the controversial status of the doctrine from the learner by presenting it as though it were a fact, but Hull distinguishes indoctrination from evangelization. In the latter the intention is to persuade, even though the techniques might be close to those of the indoctrinator.[14]

None of these commentators, interestingly, raises the question of whether indoctrination by omission is also possible. A child from a home in which religion and God are never mentioned and encountering a curriculum in which they do not occur, except perhaps *en passant* in history lessons, may not only have no belief in God, but may view the entire question of God as unnecessary and irrelevant, even incomprehensible. How much 'choice' has such a child had in forming this view? Such curricula exist, not in the former – officially atheist – countries of the old Soviet bloc, but in democratic English-speaking 'free' countries like New Zealand. Surely this too is indoctrination, as it has very effectively fixed habits and dispositions without engaging the child's active powers. The child genuinely means it when she says that she does not believe in God, that God is unnecessary. She has no ability to critique this view or to see how it has been so successfully implanted. In every way this fits the categories for indoctrination we have identified above, except that it is done by omission and not always with intention. But the end result is the same – a closed mind, which sincerely believes in its own programming. This is a sinister capture of integrity, because the person makes the statements with meaning and conviction. The 'doctrine' in this case is not a religious creed, but the value that religion is not important or the belief in 'no God'. It should be recognized for what it is, an anti-creed.

In the USA, commentary on indoctrination has tended to emphasize it as a method of teaching rather than as the content or intention of teaching. Church schools there are periodically accused of indoctrination,[15] but illogically, public schools, i.e. 'state schools', as they are often inaccurately known in Britain (no school is directly controlled centrally by the state), are not accused of the mirror image, secular indoctrination. It is too often presumed that the non-religious institution is value free. But no corporation or institution, secular or religious, is value free. J. P. White can find in history teaching the potential for indoctrination in the choice of content (the syllabus) and the teaching method, but like many commentators, he finds indoctrination essentially in the field of religion:

In religious education, as in history, there is also a danger that a pupil who identifies with a teacher who is a believer will be indoctrinated . . .[16]

But White is apparently unaware of the equal possibility of a pupil who identifies with a teacher who is a non-believer being indoctrinated. He is also extremely limited in arguing that the only intention a teacher in RE can have is to inculcate belief. This strange limitation only to see indoctrination in relation to religion is shared by Tasos Kazepides:

> Ayatollahs, evangelists and bishops are not interested in indoctrination in general, because there is no such thing, but in the inculcation of specific doctrines that are foundational to their respective ways of life.[17]

But why not also include the communists of North Korea and China and the members of the National Secular Society in their eagerness to inculcate atheistic beliefs and values? One might make the preliminary observation that good religious education, as opposed to religious instruction, will always be de-indoctrinatory, because it will increase pupil choice. Harvey Siegel takes a wider view, acknowledging that even science can indoctrinate.[18]

While European history has made westerners very cautious about the dangers of religious indoctrination, they are culturally less ready to receive and examine evidence for secular indoctrination. Religion, particularly the Christian religion, is frequently put in the dock, but secular worldviews are rarely subjected to the same public scrutiny. The spotlight is shining on religious indoctrination when it ought to be turned equally on the secular. Even at the outset of the discussion, therefore, we can clearly trace a cultural tradition of viewing indoctrination as restricted to pro-religious activities or intentions. Anti-religious activities and intentions have escaped the attention of leading commentators – and therefore escaped inclusion in the received understanding of what indoctrination is. The main report of the FARE project sums indoctrination up well, in arguing that it occurs in education when 'pupils are given one view of the world in such a way that they are unable to see any other'.[19] As far as religion goes, is it not the case that most westerners cannot 'see' a religious view of the world? This looks suspicious. Who or what has given them this view? On what authority? Might secularization be the culprit?

Secularization

Secularization is the process whereby religious institutions and practices become peripheral or almost invisible in a society in which they were or were perceived to be central and pivotal. E. Bailey offers some important observations on its origins.[20] Originally, to be secular meant to be released from 'religious status', e.g. when a member of the clergy left their religious order such as the Benedictines to serve as 'secular clergy', as a parish priest not under the direct rule or governance of the order or monastery. In this sense the word 'religious' is still infrequently used to mean a member of an order (*religio* = the canon or rule of the order), e.g. 'she is a religious', a nun. After the dissolution of the monasteries in England (1535–9) the word 'religious' transferred to churches. So although 'secular' originally meant non-monastic, it came to mean non-ecclesiastical. The University of Exeter, in which I work, is in that sense a secular university. It is not founded, funded or controlled by the church, though it maintains theology and religious education within its portfolio for teaching and research. John Calvin uses the term in this sense. He expects the secular government to support religion as well as exercise a welfare function and defend the peace.[21] Bailey points out that the meaning of secular is always dependent on the meaning of religious. So, like a seesaw, as the religious declines, the secular increases and *vice versa*. Owen Chadwick puts it another way: there never was 'a dream-society that once upon a time was not secular'.[22]

Secularism, in contrast, is the philosophy or mindset that seeks actively to advance secularization, to remove all religious points of reference, belief and practice from life. Secularists are the atheistic evangelists of secularization, although not all atheists are secularists. Secularists remain a vocal, even strident, articulate yet tiny minority in British society. For the religious institutions themselves the process of secularization has been traumatic and demoralizing. 'Tacitly modern society simply denies the authority of the Churches, by ignoring them.'[23] This can produce reactions of panic: 'What can we do to win people back?' These reactions, which can lead to crass quick-fix results like 'Get guitars into worship', are almost always, like all panic, unhelpful. Nothing can be more pathetic than religious agencies trying to 'get with it' for the wrong reasons. Secularization can produce reactions of retreat: 'We survivors shall huddle more closely together in the ghetto, consoling ourselves with the old stories, and hoping for better times.' It can equally lead to the 'head in the sand' syndrome: 'Crisis – what crisis?' Secularization can also produce modernization of beliefs, rituals and morals and a sort of eclecticism, which imports elements from other cultures and subcultures.[24]

It is possible to trace the whole process by which a society like the UK, whose cultures, education and legal systems, art, architecture, literature, music, sculpture and moral values have been shaped largely by Christianity, has apparently so easily and swiftly discarded it. People 'did not miss the gentle influence of religion in the life of the nation'.[25] Bonhoeffer, in a prison letter written on 16 July 1944, sees secularization as a long and inevitable process in history which can be traced back to a range of people including Herbert of Cherbury, Montaigne, Machiavelli, Grotius, Descartes, Spinoza, Kant, Fichte, Nicolas of Cusa and Giordano Bruno. Secularization is linked directly with his concept of the autonomy of humankind, humankind come of age, no longer needing the 'prop' of religion. God as a working hypothesis in morals, politics, or science, is surmounted and abolished. A. D. Gilbert also sees secularization as the product of a long process, in which the Christian worldview moves from a position of being normative, to one of being dominant and then to one of being marginal. J. Byrne pinpoints the period between Descartes and Kant as laying the intellectual foundations, 'the scalpel of reason', for the widespread secularization of western society in the twentieth century.[26] For E. L. Mascall 'secular' means that whole body of thought and activity connected with what is sometimes called 'this world' – it excludes considerations of life after death and of a transcendent reality that cuts into this world.[27] It also alleges that this world is complete, all we have, not antecedent to another order or existence which somehow validates it. This is an important insight. Secularization is not merely a social phenomenon, e.g. falling numbers in church attendance, but also a mental or intellectual one in which people appear not only to live happily without recourse to religion, but to *think* without recourse to it as well.

Towler and Coxon see secularization in England working in three historical phases.[28] The first was in Tudor England, with the dissolution of the monasteries and the creation of the Church of England, after which the only non-religious control exercised by the churches was over education. The second phase was the Victorian era, when the churches lost overall control of education, and the clergy lost their social influence and status. In the third phase, the closing decades of the twentieth century, the Church moved from being 'an important and central voluntary organization to one on the margin of social life' and doubts arose about the role of the clergy as a profession. Arnold Toynbee sees the roots of secularization in the seventeenth century, in which technology started to replace religion after the destructiveness of religious fanaticism in the English Civil War.[29] For John Wolffe, secularization is well described by the term 'oscillation': the dry eighteenth century is replaced by nineteenth-century religious fervour which in turn gives way, post-Darwin and biblical criticism, to twentieth-century decline. Resurgence may lie ahead.[30] Adrian Hastings sees this same oscillation with the tenth, thirteenth, seventeenth and nineteenth centuries as the times of religious advance. 'Only when religion has adjusted itself to that expulsion [from wider social control and being domesticated by the state] can it effectively resume its missionary task.'[31] He concedes that the 'business of religion in the West seems perilous enough'. But the field of secularization is rather like a hall of mirrors. Things are not always what they appear.

For Gilbert, Protestant Christianity is peculiarly liable to secularization – and Protestant Christianity has been the cultural norm in England. This is because it has no enduring structure of authority and its leaders are personalities rather than hierarchical office holders such as archbishops; its lay or democratic systems provide a vehicle for the autonomy of humankind and its involvement in modernization and capitalism has not been happy. Protestant attempts to combine positive attitudes towards worldly success (the work ethic) with negative attitudes to worldliness have led in the end to a mundane, bourgeois complacency.[32] One might add that a sense of urgent, purposeful working for the Kingdom of God does not come over in such congregations. For P. L. Berger, there is an intimate causal connection between pluralism and secularization. Religion loses its public hold and people increasingly regard it as a private choice where there is plurality.[33] Pluralism is 'an attitude that despairs of any possible access to truth' and modernity leads to uncertainty even on questions as basic as 'Who am I?'[34] Berger, like Gilbert, sees Protestantism as very vulnerable. For Protestantism is 'a radical truncation, a reduction to "essentials" at the expense of a vast wealth of religious contents . . . an immense shrinkage in the scope of the sacred . . . The sacred apparatus is reduced to a minimum and, even there, divested of its more numinous qualities.'[35] The Protestant believer no longer lives in a world 'ongoingly penetrated by the sacred'.

Berger's view could be restated in theological terms. Protestantism is a reduction: its doctrine is shorn of 'Romish superstition' and accretions and the decapitated statues and vandalized rood screens of its pre-Reformation churches witness mutely to this purge. 'Liberal Protestantism' can be seen as one reduction further. For example, you not only do away with devotions to the Virgin Mary as an over-exalted Roman mistake, but also with the Virgin Birth itself, often on *a priori* rationalist grounds that miracles do not happen. Secularization arises much more naturally out of Liberal Protestantism, which has embraced rationalism as its guiding star. D. F. Strauss, although he might be seen as the progenitor of the Liberal Protestant tradition, also undermines it by dissolving the supernatural and spiritual elements. The onion of belief has been pared away to reveal – nothing! His admirer Don Cupitt is left only with death as the final end and the non-self as the goal. This is classic reductionism. Berger notes that evangelical Protestantism, in common with Islam, has avoided this particular trap and reacted against modernity, which he sees as the product of Hebrew religiosity and Greek reason.

John Habgood views the privatization of religion as symptomatic of our time.[36] A nuclear family is separated from its other relatives. Mother and father go to separate places of work, the children to (often) large schools. The family shops in the supermarket and goes around in their private capsule or car. The public world is encountered only through the medium of their TV, viewed in private and derived from channels of their choosing. This is post-modern, in that we decide what is 'real' and try to find meaning for ourselves as individuals in a world which, objectively viewed, has no meaning. Habgood is another commentator who notes the secularization of the mind, as distinct from that of institutions.[37] He relates this to subtle changes in consciousness, not a straightforward loss of belief in the supernatural or astrology or 'pseudo-scientific mythologies', but rather a narrowing of consciousness in which religion is no longer attacked but ignored.

Put another way by Gilbert, people have become tone deaf to any orchestration of religious dogmas.[38] Chadwick notes that 'we may have less sense of providence in our lives'.[39] Bailey, more cheerfully for religion, notes that the secularization thesis is long past its 'golden summer', which he identifies as the 1960s.[40] The organized religions in his view are possibly indestructible and 'we can never be sure what "form" the religion will take'.[41] We shall consider in Chapter 3 the ways in which the secularization thesis is deeply flawed and does not account for the persistence of religions in the UK. But Bailey is wrong about immortal religions. Religions *do* die. Ancient Egypt and ancient Greece provide two examples that offer no comfort to any religion in decline. S. Akhtar qualifies this view: religions do not die in the ways that individuals do, but have that elusive power to live and live on as races do.[42] He advises caution in staking money on the death of religion.

Perhaps the most appropriate symbol of the secularization of British society is the supermarket. Its architecture may include turrets or other ornamentation redolent of cathedrals or at least indicating a building of some significance (compare the mock Gothic cathedral that is London's St Pancras Station as the Victorian equivalent in this secularization process). In the supermarket we can satisfy all our needs: food, clothing, pharmaceuticals, contraception, banking, finance and insurance, newspapers and magazines, entertainment via CDs and DVDs, computers and the internet, electrical appliances, furniture, car accessories and petrol. We can buy National Lottery tickets with their promise of the chance of a future different only in the boundlessness of its material possibilities. Some supermarkets have crèche facilities to allow us to go around more easily and some offer funeral packages and facilities for making wills. The people at the check-out say hello and offer to summon help packing our bags, so they must be our friends. We in return can show our loyalty by using special cards that mean that the larger the sums we pay the supermarket, the more tiny bonuses we receive in return. Truly from our first nappy to the grave and the flowers to go on it, the supermarket has become our great provider. Unlike the churches, it is always, or nearly always, open.

Shopping is no longer a utilitarian pursuit concerned with collecting the things we need. It is about acquiring a range of foods, clothes, furniture and décor, to enable 'Me' to make personal statements about myself in every department of life – except the religious, which is strictly 'private'. Tiny toddlers, already clad in name-brand jeans and little trainers, are brought up to shop from the earliest age. As soon as children have spending power, shopping is one of the first independent activities they undertake, as an expression of their selves, in distinction to the identity of their parents. Yet in another sense, shopping is not about personal expression at all. We are all 'led', interestingly a term with religious currency as well, by the right designer label, the expert ploys of the advertiser and what the football or pop stars or supermodels are wearing. But they in turn are paid a lot of money to wear these clothes. There is not much real freedom of choice.

The other aspect of modern life which has gone unnoticed in the mapping of secularization is the effect of indoor living on the way we think. In ancient times, as in many parts of the world even now, humankind lived outdoors. Life was not idyllic, but it was punctuated by the seasons and by closeness to and awareness of nature – certainly not a romanticized view of nature and the living planet. Nobody could find romantic Flora Thompson's account, in *Lark Rise to Candleford*, of the killing of the village pig.[43] But now people live most of their lives indoors. For some people even exercise is an indoor activity carried out at a fitness club to which they drive. In warm, protected, indoor environments we feel safe, confident and in control. It is only when a hurricane rips the roof off our house (as occurred in southern England in 1987) or the hurricane of a relationship break-up rips the roof off our life that we see that this worldview is a flawed one. A well-stocked freezer and warm central heating will not cushion us from bereavement. Private health insurance cannot prevent serious illness. But for most of the time, we don't see that and just get on with our secure indoor life. We can see 'nature' on TV if we choose, or through the window of our air-conditioned car or in the pages of a lavishly illustrated coffee-table book. If the central heating breaks down we do not pray to God for help. Instead, we telephone the central-heating engineer. With the supermarket and the central-heating engineer to attend to our needs and keep us cosy, who needs God? On an everyday basis, society reassures us that we may safely press the Delete key on religion. Does education do the same?

Education

'Education' means different things. In its many institutional forms, it is a vast enterprise, in theory from cradle to grave, employing many hundreds of thousands of people in the UK alone and catering for millions of children and adult clients or consumers. As an academic discipline, e.g. in universities, the precise nature of education is unclear. It is often assumed to be a sub-branch of the social sciences and is presumed naturally to use empirical research methodology. At other times education looks like an umbrella term for different disciplines: the history of education, philosophy of education, curriculum development, child psychology, school management studies, etc. This usage is similar to 'Arts'. As a factor in the UK economy, education is massive. It gobbles billions of pounds. It keeps many young people out of the labour market post-16 for five years at least. It is presumed, not always correctly, to bring riches to its better-qualified alumni: graduates. It also brings increasing debt to its undergraduate consumers. As a political factor, education is rarely out of public scrutiny and debate, about raising standards or reorganizing some aspect of it. The secretary of state for education is a senior government minister, who obtains easy publicity by virtue of the job. Politicians are apt to speak about education with Messiah-like status. They proclaim what 'needs to be done', presumably either simply because they once went to school or because they can see that, potentially, education moulds minds.

But what values is education assuming or affirming and how far do the 11 years' captivity of compulsory schooling and the five years of frequently extended sentence (post-16 studies plus degree) shape minds? If a society's education is in some ways a mirror of its values, what do we see in the mirror of education as a reflection of our society? In the UK we are not yet ready to see education as a product of culture. This is myopic. For instance, in Britain the school-teacher is *not* a respected figure, treated deferentially by pupils and their parents. Instead, children are encultured to 'try it on'. This would be a strange ritual, if it were not so familiar. Classes will challenge teachers in the early weeks of encounter. September is the trysting season (unless a new teacher arrives mid-year). Teachers are expected to respond rather like lion tamers and growl and threaten with a mixture of bravado and bluff. The class then ritually submits. It despises those teachers who do not bring it to heel.

But in many schools a minority of genuinely disturbed children and their less disturbed but more wily peer group imitators are allowed to continue to make life awkward for the teacher and slow down the progress of the lesson. Just one such child in a class is sufficient to cause major disruption and delay. The current politically correct mantra of 'inclusion' does not allow them to be dealt with firmly, or to be rapidly excluded from the class. So they have to be coaxed and begged and cajoled, while meanwhile they torment the teacher and expect not to conform to the rules that apply to the other children. Do these children know the time-honoured 'difference between right and wrong'? I never met one who did not. But things are said by children to teachers, and done in lessons, which would be allowed to happen in few other parts of society. What has happened to the rights of the teacher to teach and the rights of the other children in the class to be taught?

All this is encultured behaviour. It is not inevitable – genetic – and it is not global adolescent behaviour. 'Humankind come of age' has produced unruly children in the west. In the process of transition of the teacher's role from feared despot, cane in hand, to professional friend, respect has evaporated somewhere along the line. Children lost their fear of teachers, in the main, which was a gain. But they did not retain their respect, in the main, which was a big loss. The reality is that British society has allowed, even encouraged, this change in pupil–teacher relationship to happen and has now come not just to accept but to expect this behaviour pattern as the norm. Most professionals and consumers (i.e. teachers, parents and children) are not even consciously aware that this has happened. The media response oscillates between blaming teachers for losing their grip and blaming parents for abdicating their responsibilities. A rights culture has paradoxically reduced the rights of the teacher and ignored the rights of the majority of the class.

But if that is what education has become culturally in many classrooms, what is education, philosophically conceived? For John Hull,

education is distinguishable from learning, which is a broader concept.[44] If I fall down a hole in the road I may say that I need to learn
to look where I am going, but such learning does not constitute education. Education can also be distinguished from training. Human
beings, according to Hull, can be educated and trained, but animals
can only be trained. Training involves acquired responses in certain
situations. Education involves an understanding of the principles on
which skills are based. Interestingly, recent British governments
have decided that teachers should be trained, no longer 'educated', a
reversion to Victorian language and thinking. Student teachers are
called 'trainees' in all official documentation from the Teacher
Training Agency to university departments of education and local
schools. This implies that teaching is a set of skills like plumbing in
which you can be tested and certified. The fact that the plumber is
frequently better paid than the teacher is another social comment on
British culture.

For C. S. Lewis education is 'only the most fully conscious of the
channels whereby each generation influences the next . . . A man
whose mind was formed in a period of cynicism and disillusion, cannot teach hope or fortitude.'[45] E. Gill is clear that the teacher's business is to draw out of pupils the knowledge they already have and
help them to organize it in such a way that instead of being frag-
mentary and unrelated, it becomes 'a satisfactory "picture" of reality'.[46] W. R. Niblett implies that education is concerned with 'a
committed way of life'[47] but points out that since the surest things in
a world of uncertainties are material possessions, we are in danger of
gearing our education towards materialism. For R. S. Peters, education is more than a skill or skills. It involves a body of knowledge
and some kind of schematization to raise it above the level of unrelated facts. It also transforms, by influencing the way an educated
person responds to stimuli around them, e.g. a historic building or
city. It implies an ability to critique fields of expertise and also the
possession of 'cognitive perspective,' the ability to connect areas of
expertise with the wider whole. There is a big difference between
being knowledgeable and being educated. The former might enable
one to perform well in pub quiz teams or the board game Trivial
Pursuit. The latter is almost a way of life, affecting one's responses
and decisions in many situations, just like religion.

A conflict of expectation about education on the part of various interest groups may also cloud an understanding of what it is. What politicians want education to achieve may differ from the views of professional educators, which in turn might diverge from the views of parents and the possibly different views of their own children. One of the dangers in the present UK education system is that in order to keep jumping through the hoops of frequent testing and examinations, Ofsted inspection, quality-assurance procedures, league tables, publicity, etc., all other aims for education may be buried under six feet of paper. Danger is not too strong a word for this situation. For the frenzy of compliance with the dictates of government might result in two consequences: a real lowering of standards, under the cloak of meeting paper targets; and a lack of concern for the values being transmitted through the whole process. The first consequence is not unusual. Teachers desperate to get their students A grades, both for the benefit of the students themselves and for the glory of the school under inspection or league-table pressures, or to gain their own promotion, undertake a lot of intense coaching and 'spoon-feeding'. The resultant grades please everyone involved, but they must be seen as detrimental in many ways to real education. In such a pressured situation, the students expect 'education' to be given to them on a plate. They become passive rather than proactive and it is hard to see how the old-fashioned quality of love of learning can be engendered in this process. In such a situation education is a commodity the student expects the teacher to deliver to them, neatly packaged, in a way that absolves the student from responsibility, except to digest it. The second consequence is that those involved in the education process are so busy working towards measurable 'results' that the invisible conditioning, the subterranean values, go unconsidered. If you want to subvert an organization, simply keep its employees frantically busy doing tasks that do not, ultimately, matter. Make their pay, promotion and job security dependent on these tasks and they will be far too busy to question anything. Has this happened to British schooling?

Education at present is much better at identifying its short-term or medium-term goals than its long-term aims. It is easy to say when teaching maths to a Year 9 (age 13+) middle-ability set what attainment target the teacher is aiming to meet and what the specific intended learning outcomes for that particular lesson are. Similarly, in an Open University tutorial with an undergraduate class of age range of perhaps 23 to 70, there will be specific issues arising from course broadcasts and written texts to check, discuss and relate to the next assignment, with perhaps feedback from the marking of the previous assignment. Teachers in that sense are clearly focused individuals, more so than a generation ago when teaching objectives were often not specific and many lessons appeared aimless. Today's teachers and tutors are adept at achieving curriculum learning targets with their students. What is much less common is to see oneself as part of the wider process of education and to ask what that means.

There is an ongoing debate on 'graduateness' and in what it consists which illustrates excellently the problem of British educational aims. Graduateness was never formally defined, but by custom and tradition it used to be based on residence, reading and time. You resided in or near your chosen university for three years and you read books, as well as attending sessions for lectures, labs or tutorials. The guided reading with tutorial support made students proactive in their learning. Residence on campus in a hall for at least part of the three years and living away from home were seen as an integral part of the 18-year-old student's education. The course of study, although vitally important, was only one aspect of the process. But all this gradually changed, in a typically British piecemeal fashion. The privately funded University of Buckingham introduced two-year degrees. Undergraduates of the Open University, all part time, did not have the option of residence, except for intensive summer schools. In any university, mature students did not want to live in halls away from their home. Halls themselves changed in character, with noise and alcohol abuse becoming major problems, while pallid attempts to ape the Oxbridge colleges and produce a sort of hall culture and hall-based social life were abandoned. When the age of majority fell from 21 to 18, it became even harder to impose discipline on student excesses. Halls became just places to sleep in, provided the noise was not too loud.

Mature students increasingly wanted the option of completing a degree part time over five or six years in some cases, so that undergraduate degrees now became a matter of stacking up module credits rather than completing a course of study in three fixed years. Increasing student debt meant that more students chose to live at home and attend their local university as day students rather than incur residence debts further afield, perhaps on superior courses.

Many undergraduates had to take on part-time paid work during term time as well as vacations to make ends meet. 'Reading around' the subject became virtually unknown. Learning became ruthlessly focused on the next assignment. To the rather archaic question 'What are you reading at university?' the real answer is often – the minimum.

Most significant of all, the British graduate ceased to be a privileged person, 10 per cent of the population, with expectations of a job and income to reflect this position. With the pressure towards 50 per cent entry to university, the first degree for many has become a sort of finishing school, merely an extension of the sixth-form conveyor belt, rather than a course of study chosen for academic or careerist reasons. Now two-year 'degrees' are envisaged for vocational subjects. What does it mean to graduate BEng (Plumbing) in two years compared to a Scottish four-year MA in, say, English Literature? How can we compare these 'degrees'? What a mess it all is. The only real common denominator now to most first degrees is that they are a form of post-18 education.

'Graduateness' is only one aspect of education. It is not the story of a move from the good old past to the bad old present, but of inevitable change which British society was ill-equipped to manage because it had no view of 'education', no forum to examine the issues, no agreed principles and no plan. It illustrates how easily attempts to define or refine any part of the education system can come unstuck when there is no supporting national tradition of considering the whole enterprise and attempting to provide a rationale acceptable not only to the educated, but across society as a whole. What happened instead was political meddling, accompanied by a media debate, conducted at a trivial level, about tuition fees: whether the refuse collector should pay for the doctor's education. In such a confused situation for education, it is quite possible that the system could contain values that were never debated, never openly adopted, never canvassed. Secular indoctrination could easily occur in this sort of confused culture of education. Who would notice if it did?

Having identified some of the meanings attaching to indoctrination, secularization and education, we are now in a position to examine those trends in British society, and English society in particular, which have shaped attitudes to religion. But do we need first to define religion? Or what we mean by God? The task would be enormous, but a note on how the term 'religion' is used in this book will help to clarify and close this introduction to the story. In a world in which we see only religions, it is very difficult to define religion in the singular. There is certainly no evidence in favour of some sort of higher essence or distillation from religions that can be refined into pure religion. Those who maintain in conversation that 'all religions are basically the same', a proposition that is harder to defend the more closely one examines it, might wish to distil a higher essence; often they are asserting the commonality among religions to be love of one's neighbour, i.e. morality. But the essence of religions is not morality; a moral code is one manifestation of a religion. Islam, for example, has a moral code. However, Islam is not primarily morality, but an acceptance of Allah's One-ness. Islamic morality flows from the implications of obeying One God.

For the purposes of this book we take religions to be those complex spiritual, communal, social, ethnographic, theological organisms and ways of life that are generally understood as such: Zoroastrianism, Baha'i, Jainism, Judaism, Hinduism, etc. Where the word 'religion' is used in the singular in the chapters that follow it does not imply a higher essence derived from this multiplicity of religions, but rather any religious way of life as opposed to a non-religious or atheistic or secular life stance. As for God, at this stage we might note that British children sometimes discuss, or are invited by teachers to discuss, whether they believe 'in' God. This question is loaded against God and religion for various reasons. One is that whoever or whatever God may be, God is not an object like a distant planet or a UFO or an alleged Queen Anne chair, that one 'believes in' or not according to evidence and the exercise of a sort of personal choice. Another way in which the question is loaded is that it turns God into a quiz-show contestant. God is put on the spot and challenged to prove his or her existence in order to gain the prize of our belief; so God's existence depends on our belief, upon whether we accredit or reward God or not. This is humanistic to the point of arrogance. Ultimate questions call for greater humility of inquiry and willingness to examine the ways in which questions are conceived and worded so as sometimes to restrict answers.

We are perfectly entitled to ask as many searching questions as we like about God and who or what God is presumed to be, using the

brains that religious people would claim God gave us. We are perfectly entitled on the grounds of intellectual argument or personal
experience to reject the possibility of God entirely. But we ought
also to consider the possibility that God is real and that we ourselves
are products of a culture that discourages belief. In other words, we
need to scrutinize reasons, experiences and cultural climates that
lead to unbelief as well as the claims of belief. What have we done
to religion in Britain, in society and in our schools?

2

The Choking Cradle?:
Religion Under Threat in English Society

If a process is at work that is indoctrinating people, particularly children growing up in Britain, against religion, we have to consider the society into which babies are born and the worldview that they imbibe along with their breast milk. Currently it is a choking cradle in terms of their likelihood to form, or even understand, a religious view of life.

English society has a long history of ambivalence towards religion

Many more people attended church in 1901, the year of Queen Victoria's death, than in 1837 when she came to the throne, but they were fewer as a percentage of the total population. By 1901 agnosticism and atheism had 'come out'. The unchurched, especially the intellectual unchurched, were visible and vocal in a way in which they had not been at the start of Victoria's long reign.

In 1851 a national census on religion was attempted by Horace Mann, an agent employed by the registrar-general. Statistically the returns from this census are messy, but it is possible to glean some information from them. There were no individual returns, only institutional. Mann's office sent a form to the minister of each recorded place of worship, on the basis of lists provided by the census district enumerator. Census Sunday was 30 March 1851 and the method employed was a head count at each act of worship. Despite reminders, 989 out of 14,077 Anglican places of worship did not respond. The analysis of the results appeared in 1854. The total population of England and Wales was 17,929,609. Church of England attendance on census Sunday totalled 5,292,551, that of Roman Catholics 383,630, Nonconformists 5,219,885.

At the time this was a seismic shock for the Anglicans. Nonconformity had almost overtaken them and the census results gave momentum to political attempts to attack established church privilege. But Mann had no mechanism for identifying 'twicers' or 'thricers', people who attended church more than once, of whom nonconformity certainly had more than the Church of England. He estimated that only 7,261,032 out of the 10,896,066 attendances were real people. Mann's statistics might mean that even in 1851, less than 50 per cent of the nation attended church. What is significant for us now is that what many assume to be the Victorian golden age of churchgoing, in which 'everyone' went to church, never existed. A very large section of the population was outside the churches even in 1851, before Darwin, the rise of 'biblical criticism' and the so-called Victorian 'loss of faith'.[1] Unfortunately, the whole idea of a religious census proved so controversial that although it was discussed again in every decade up to 1910, it was not revived until 2001. So the proposition that the UK has moved from a position of almost universal church attendance to almost zero church attendance is untrue in both respects.

Chadwick notes the origins of the word 'secularization' in late Victorian England, admitting that the truth it undoubtedly conveys is hard to define.[2] *The Secular Review*, edited for a time by George Jacob Holyoake, attributed the coining of the related word 'secularism' to its editor in 1876. Holyoake defined it almost in credal terms as 'the study of promoting human welfare by material means; the utilitarian rule to measure human welfare by; and making the service of others a duty of life . . . It replaces theology.'[3] The journal carried another secularist's view of secularism: all action can be based on human experience; 'science is the practical guide of life'; to prevent evils in the world 'study the order of Nature and act accordingly'; intelligent actions turn evils (e.g. floods) to good (e.g. irrigation). Finally, 'work is worship', a secularization of the Protestant work ethic.[4] It was in many ways the logical climax of a process of attacks by intellectuals and some less educated people on religion, using weapons provided courtesy of the Enlightenment.[5] Part of this process was the social realization that atheists were perfectly capable of leading morally good lives. In previous centuries, atheism had often been closely linked with immorality in the public mind.

If secularism was now a visible lobby, the rise of cycling clubs and golf clubs made the secularization of Sunday obvious. F. Meyrick could write in 1902 that 'pleasure seeking' was 'robbing us of our Sunday', that an alliance of unbelievers, deists, atheists and agnostics was trying 'to *free* [my italics] the day from its religious character and make it primarily . . . for enjoyment and secular pleasure'.[6] Freedom and religion were seen in conflict, which was characteristic of the western approach to religion: religion was seen as limiting, restrictive, restraining. Meyrick viewed liberal clergy as complicit in de-restricting Sunday. W. B. Trevelyan could write in 1903 that in the 'last twenty years' the English Sunday had lost its 'old fashioned quiet' because more people were travelling and entertaining friends.[7] 'The age is an unduly busy one: over-activity is the fashionable vice . . . and as a result, many lives remain stunted and undeveloped'.[8] Rural Britain, Chadwick argues, still felt itself to be Christian in 1901, though in an imprecise way. J. N. Figgis in 1911 detects 'no outward change' then.[9] The drift to the cities, however, often meant the drift from the church. The twentieth century was to confirm that move of house sometimes dislocated church allegiance and was more common than loss of faith in accounting for some of the drift away from the churches. Churchgoing was associated with 'where we used to live'.

The city itself was different from the superficially unchanging rural scene. Here secular halls and labour churches were competing with chapels and churches for the attention of the aspiring working class, which was now literate, organized and increasingly powerful. Since the late eighteenth century, Edward Gibbon had enabled intellectuals to snigger at Christian history while David Hume allowed them to scoff at the implausibility of the famous 'proofs' of God's existence. By the late nineteenth century, high-profile figures were known not to be Christian, even if the detailed story of their loss of faith reads more like bereavement than adventure or discovery: Thomas Carlyle, Charles Darwin, George Eliot, Thomas Hardy, Beatrix Potter, Leslie Stephen. They were seldom secularists, sometimes not even full-blown atheists, but they were palpably not traditional believers, and contemporary attempts by some believers to claim that, say, Darwin was 'really a Christian' underneath were ignoble and unfounded. At a meeting of the Metaphysical Society, Thomas Huxley coined the term that was to describe the position he held, neither atheism nor theism, which reflected his view that the God-question was insoluble: 'agnostic'.[10] All this signified the start of a phase of British public life sometimes inaccurately labelled 'loss of faith'. For some it was actually a reformulation of faith into something much less doctrinal and rather more experiential. But in some intellectual circles, unbelief began to look inevitable.

Loss of faith became the preoccupation of novels, notably Mary Humphry Ward's *Robert Elsmere*, which in its day outsold Darwin and was reviewed by Gladstone in 8,000 words. William Hale White (Mark Rutherford) explored the same theme in two semi-autobiographical novels.[11] Do novels reflect public moods or do they create them? Perhaps there is an element of both. Kingsley, Dickens and Disraeli could arouse social conscience in novels. A. L. Drummond argues that novels tend to elevate character above creed, implying that they will always tend towards the unorthodox.[12] *Robert Elsmere* is a long and badly written novel, tedious to the modern reader even in the shortened form imposed upon its author by her publisher. But it obviously touched on a leading concern of those Victorians who read novels. The ethical dilemma of a clergyman who loses his faith and has to decide whether to resign his livelihood, losing his income and his home as a result, but protecting his integrity, was a compelling story line.

In a celebrated 'real life' case a leading Unitarian minister, Moncure Conway, took his congregation close to agnosticism with his attacks on traditional Christianity and the warm welcome he gave to non-Christian speakers at services. Inscribed on the chapel walls were the names of Jesus, Solomon, Zoroaster, Socrates, Buddha, Confucius, Plato, Muhammad, Omar Khayyam, Shakespeare, Spinoza, Bacon, Bruno, George Fox, Voltaire, Paine and Goethe. Soon after Conway moved on, the chapel reconstituted itself as South Place Ethical Society, abandoning even its residual theism.[13] Now in a different location, honouring Conway's contribution in the name Conway Hall, its members claim to be 'the oldest free thought community in the world'. They trace their history through stages from the society's origin in 1793: loss of belief in an eternal hell, then loss of belief in the Trinity, finally the renunciation of God in 1888. Ironically this was the same year in which the Church of England approved the Lambeth Quadrilateral, formulating what it regarded as the essential basis for a reunited church: scripture as containing 'all things necessary to salvation', the Apostles' Creed, the sacraments of baptism and eucharist and the 'historic episcopate'. The Quadrilateral's proponents did not appear to appreciate that the wolf was at the door.

Atheism was 'coming out' in other ways by the 1880s. From 1886 atheists could sit in the House of Commons. Again, atheism was seen to win a nationally publicized legal battle, which made it look as if Christianity was simply clinging on to ancient power and privilege. This case involved the election and subsequent re-election of Charles Bradlaugh as Northampton's MP, his refusal to swear the oath of allegiance and even his imprisonment before the law was eventually changed. By late Victorian times the press was treating religion 'as if from outside'.[14] The sermons of the great Victorian preachers were not printed in the secular press. Moreover, the political threat to the establishment of the Church of England from nonconformist pressure was still real. John Gay argues that even by the 1880s the Church of England had been drifting from the centre of national life for 200 years.[15] The universities were ceasing to be seen as Christian institutions. The recently opened London University was not religious even at its foundation. The clerical stranglehold on Fellowships at Oxford and Cambridge was broken. Headteachers of boys' public schools were much less likely to be ordained than a generation earlier. Science was no longer a clerically dominated hobby but a rising profession. Although nonconformists did not realize it, their membership and influence had peaked by 1901 and were set to decline throughout the twentieth century. Nevertheless, 'whether or not the citizens attended those churches or chapels [built by the Victorians], the Victorians preserved a country which was powerfully influenced by Christian ideas and continued to accept the Christian ethic as the highest known'.[16] But that influence was fading.

Chadwick argues that by the end of the nineteenth century, the European working classes were 'somewhere between unconscious secularist and unconscious Christian'. They attended church for rites of passage, but identified the clergy and the church with the political Right and with a different and alien social class.[17] Nor were they orthodox in doctrine; social workers among the poor reported that they laughed at the idea of hell. By 1911 Figgis could write that 'it is scarcely too much to say that English society is ceasing to be

Christian',[18] not by revolt but as a result of indifference and uncertainty. He could also pinpoint that the problem lay with

> that mass of people who . . . are not unbelievers, but they have a vague notion that the foundations are rotten, or at least not sufficiently secure for them to act with any vigour . . . People will not take things for granted as they did, and in their perplexity they are apt to leave it all alone . . . In the old days this vagueness inclined people to a general conformity . . . Nowadays there are plenty of alternatives in educated society, and the English vagueness, enhanced by the notion of a universal religious sentiment, as revealed by Comparative Religion, tends to make people regard definite Christian teaching as merely a form of the religious spirit which has nothing in it supernatural or authoritative. Hence arises an indifference to all genuine religious knowledge and something like hostility to the claims of the Church.[19]

Long before Berger *et al.*, Figgis identified pluralism as a possible cause of loss of belief. (We shall see in Chapter 3 that this 'mass of people' was to remain curiously loyal to Christianity over the next century.) For Figgis, Christianity had been domesticated and turned into a negative moral force in English society. 'Nowadays it presents itself as a sort of glorified policeman, bidding them [the present generation] keep off the grass, and not as "the strange Man upon the Cross" calling men to the most weird of all knight-errantries.'[20] An Anglo-Catholic, Figgis nevertheless expresses admiration for the old evangelicals who understood the difference between the Church and the world, which is now too blurred for Christianity to be seen as distinctive.[21] A. N. Wilson identifies the closing decades of the nineteenth century as 'the true era' of the death of God and argues that the twentieth century opened with an atheist orthodoxy among many intellectuals.[22] Another writer comments:

> If the younger generation have never been told what the Christians say and never heard any arguments in defence of it, then their agnosticism or indifference is fully explained. There is no need to look any further: no need to talk about the general intellectual climate of the age . . .

These words are significant for various reasons. One is that they illustrate that a lot of teaching about Christianity can go on without any presentation of its truth claims, of its basic message that the God whose nature is love intervened in human history *in person* to restore humankind. Another is that although the intellectual climate might shape the way we think more than the writer in the quotation is willing to acknowledge, what children are taught at classroom level matters. But perhaps most interesting of all is that the words were written in 1948 by C. S. Lewis, in what is now presumed to have been the heyday of Christian religious education, in a country in which world religions were not considered much, if at all. The pressure from humanism for its acceptance in classrooms as a valid stance for living lay some twenty years in the future, in the mid-1960s. The book in which these words appeared was by B. G. Sandhurst – Lewis wrote the preface – and was entitled *How Heathen is Britain?* Sandhurst, who had carried out research with army cadets, noted that the teachers of 'today' were largely the undergraduates of twenty years before (around 1928). 'It is the mental climate of the Twenties that now dominates the form room'[23] and the result is that 'nearly half the young men now leaving our public and secondary schools are almost pagan'. But Sandhurst could still write, '*It is not true* [his italics] that this generation has no interest in religion.'[24] In other words, the problems which Christian-based RE faced dated back well before the 1960s. These problems were not caused by liberal Christians simply capitulating to humanist demands for syllabus space in the 1960s – as argued by Penny Thompson in her book, *Whatever Happened to Religious Education?* (2004) – or the desire to placate growing numbers of members of religions other than Christianity in the 1970s, as the Christian Right maintained in the 1980s. The problem is stated another way:

We used to think that the characteristic heresy of Anglo-Saxon Christianity was Pelagianism, but in our own day that has been superseded by a denial of the very necessity of a Church. A large proportion of English-speaking people today think of Christianity merely as a sentiment . . . Their absence from Church does not mean that they do not wish to be regarded as active followers of Christianity.[25]

In an essay titled 'Has the World Outgrown the Churches?' in a 1947 symposium, J. Middleton Murry can already perceive that a greater secularization of Christianity has occurred in Britain than in any other European country.[26] D. Woodruff argues that British Christians, apart from Roman Catholics, have no sense of belonging to an international body.[27] W. L. Andrews writes that 'most of our people' have been completely secularized 'by the economic struggle, or by the conditions of industrial life, or by a general drift of scepticism'.[28] It is the year, 1947, that is again significant. Although in 1938 the private car was the possession of a very few, such as the doctor, W. E. Sangster foresaw it as a potential threat to church attendance. Sangster is the first writer I could trace to record a claim still made by many people in the twenty-first century, that they worship God better in the beauty of the countryside in their car than 'in the dim religious light of church'.[29] The real question remains not whether they can worship in the beauty of the countryside, but whether they do. For H. G. Wood, the European churches were complicit in an intellectual and moral failure in a century that had seen two major wars in Europe and beyond. He likened this to being in the grip of a demonic power like the boy at the foot of the Mountain of Transfiguration whom the disciples could not help.[30] Frightened of upsetting 'simple believers', the Church has been silent too often when it should have been taking intellectual risks.

Post-war prosperity

The years after the Second World War saw yet more competition to religion in a society that saw real rises in the standard of living. An intellectual climate had already been created whereby it was acceptable not to be religious, perhaps laying foundations for the popular English dictum referred to on p. 2, that 'it doesn't matter what you believe, as long as you lead a good life'. Another popular mantra recorded by Rowntree and Lavers was that 'churchgoers are no better than us' or were castigated as 'hypocrites' by some non-churchgoers.[31] The Rowntree-Lavers survey raised the question whether Sunday schools might be part of the problem of children's negative attitudes towards the church rather than the solution.[32] It also detected a working-class strand of anti-clericalism. This survey of church attendance in York suggested it had fallen from 35.5 per cent

(1901) to 17.7 per cent (1935) to 13 per cent (1948). A post-war social climate was arising in which church attendance, already not the norm, increasingly had to compete with other Sunday leisure activities, as the dismantling of the late Victorian sabbatarian laws began with the opening of cinemas, public houses and shops and the holding of sporting fixtures. Rowntree and Lavers held that the Second World War had encouraged superficial living, in a situation where there was a shortage of goods and a surplus of money, and the real threat of death hung over many people. They reasoned that this superficiality, living for the moment, had carried over into the peace.

Two examples will serve to symbolize these social changes, the changing position of the privy and the rise of 24-hour shopping. In the early twentieth century, for many working-class people the privy was at the bottom of the yard or garden in an unheated shed-like building. It had no running water or electric lighting. The 'night soil man' came in the hours of darkness and removed the day's products. A generation later, the same toilet had a flush water system and per-haps electric lighting, but the winter walk down the yard in the dark was still unpleasant. A generation after that, along with the weekly bath in a portable zinc bath tub in front of the coal fire, it had been rendered unnecessary by an indoor bathroom. Within another gener-ation the bathroom had a shower as well as a bath and, for those who really wanted to splash out with their cash or credit card, a Jacuzzi and/or a bidet. Bathrooms had become lifestyle statements. All this happened within one lifetime and illustrates the move in living from convenience (!) to consumerism.

Shops changed too. In one lifetime they moved from lunch-hour closing (1 p.m. to 2 p.m.), Wednesday or Thursday half-day closure and all-day Sunday closure, plus bank-holiday and other public-hol-iday closures, including Good Friday, to seven-day opening, includ-ing 24-hour opening at some supermarkets. It is almost impossible to imagine, yet a nation with many more shift workers than today managed to shop perfectly well during such limited opening hours. This was possible partly because until the 1960s wives were often at home and grocers delivered goods more commonly than now. But the 1990s demand for Sunday opening was turned into almost a human-rights issue, the right to shop whenever one chose. It is still manifest in the frustration of those who turn up at supermarkets on Easter Day to find them closed. Having 364 days to shop is clearly not enough. The entitlement of shop workers to time off receives less publicity. This was one aspect of a paradox in British social life: people had never had so much leisure time and so many convenience gadgets, but they were always frantically busy. It became harder in schools to get children to commit to sports teams, Saturday matches and after-school practice. It became harder to enrol people in political parties, or to give up time to lead voluntary youth-work activities such as scouting and guiding. The National Lottery and the mass hobby of shopping may be expressions of real English and British national values, with out-of-town superstores as the secular cathedrals of those values.

If the activity of shopping provided competition for religious activity, then perhaps belief in the free market provided competition for belief in God. Chadwick dates the arrival of the free market in European countries to between 1860 and 1890. Liberty, which had been seen as an instrument for justice or good government, became increasingly seen as a personal possession, to enable self-realization.[33] David Jenkins analyses this change in terms of 'TINA' – There Is No Alternative to the free market – the credal statement of dogmatic authority demanding economic obedience. He links it with the fatalistic view that the free market is inevitable. Although he does not use the phrase, Jenkins' argument is that economics has become the theology of a materialist society. Markets make money. Money is the key to human prosperity, therefore 'go with the market and profit, prosperity and freedom shall be added unto you'.[34] 'Market realism . . . appears to claim that power needs no other legitimation than money, and wealth no other justification than that it has been acquired'.[35] This is a new feudalism based not on land but on money. Jenkins notes that Adam Smith associated the market with an 'invisible hand', Providence – the market is assumed to bring increased prosperity for rising numbers of the world's inhabitants. Although we have given up 'Providence' we retain an optimism about the market. But Jenkins raises questions: does it deliver? And what is the real cost, including poverty and pollution? People with unfulfilled needs but no money do not exist, as far as the market is concerned. 'The Market has been reified, and even, deified.'[36] He debunks the market as a Wizard of Oz type phenomenon, a contrivance,

a metaphor labelling a set of goings on operated by people who produce and trade; 'goings on' which are increasingly dominated by people who trade in money, by credit creation and other financial transaction . . . 'The Market' is a metaphor and the 'Free Market' is an illusion . . . [It] has become the playground of international financiers who manipulate money for further money-making and clearly have the upper hand.[37]

The media is not a friend of religion

If there is an established social tradition which is indifferent if not hostile towards religions, to what extent does the media take sides? What is its influence in shaping attitudes towards religion? An American adolescent is estimated to have clocked up 20,000 hours watching TV by the age of 16. A British young person with these viewing hours would have considerably exceeded the minimum 12,100 hours of compulsory education. The media frequently portrays religion as a source of perversion, extremism, arcane values or stupidity. Cumulatively, religion is presented as not *normal* and not *cool*. W. L. Andrews observed that since Lord Northcliffe held that religion was not news, very little appeared about it in the *Daily Mail*. But when Reginald Campbell's 'new theology' was propounded – not that there was much theology in it, as Jesus was merely an exemplar of goodness and 'Christ' is present in all people and all history – it made good copy.[38]

Chadwick notes that in the nineteenth century, public opinion was in favour of religion in a vague way but that even then, any utterance against it or unfavourable report received publicity out of all proportion to its merits. Crackpot Victorian theories about Gospel origins, like their 'Bible codes' equivalent in the twentieth century, received massive publicity and achieved high sales of books. The scholarly refutations received little note.[39] Chadwick attributes this to a law of publicity: destruction interests while construction bores.

Millions of people watch TV 'soaps'. Although religion is rarely explicitly present, soaps deal with real-life issues and at least 'keep alive the possibility of God'.[40] But ideas matter much less than feelings in a soap. When religious personnel appear in them, they suffer human dilemmas very much like the rest of us, except these caused by celibacy. S. A. Schleifer, a Muslim commentator, sees television as essentially anti-Islamic and anti-meditative, because it cannot present a person's spirituality on screen or handle the depth in a religion, religion being defined by al-Ghazali as belief in the Unseen World.[41] What cannot be seen does not make good TV. Schleifer feels that 'the entire Muslim world is rapidly being incorporated into an international secular culture based on mass communication which breaches the cultural forms that have traditionally protected Islamic consciousness'.

TV offers not only entertainment but also attitudes, implicit philosophies of life and always consumerism. A viewing audience accustomed to the BBC, which advertises only its own programmes, may not be fully aware that all other channels need to sell products via advertisements so as to generate income to produce programmes. The British debate about television has rather myopically focused on whether the BBC TV licence fee is justifiable or should be abolished in favour of subscription viewing. It ought also to embrace the implications of the financial 'licence' provided by the acquisitiveness of consumer funding for the other channels. Dorothy Sölle argues that the basic and natural human need for uniqueness, novelty and meaning has been manipulated into an obsession with possessions. 'Domination, the manipulation of consciousness, schooling in the destruction of one's own interests, are no longer performed by religion and the Church but by production and advertising. *The new religion is consumerism* [my italics].'[42] William Fore argues that television supplies pervasive myths about our society: that efficiency is the highest good; that technology is progress; that the fittest survive (they are young, white males); that those at the centre know best and should take decisions; that happiness consists of material consumption.[43] If he is right, it hardly creates a climate for spiritual or religious prosperity or for the promotion of these via the media.

Colin Morris wonders whether the fact that nearly all the material selected to appear on news programmes is bad news calls into question in the subconscious the Christian view of a loving God. J. McDonnell points out that when news stories do surface about religion, they are usually stories of social conflict: abortion, the Rushdie affair, Lebanon, inter-religious conflict in India, quarrels about women priests, church and politics in South Africa.[44] Religious doctrine, if presented at all, appears as a problem rather than a personal or communal asset. Since McDonnell wrote (1993), one could add more. There have been fierce arguments over the ordination of openly gay bishops, court cases resulting from abuse administered in some Christian Brothers schools, whether and to what extent the Roman Catholic Church has sheltered paedophile priests in the UK, the USA and Canada, and the bitter feud among Lincoln Cathedral hierarchy. 'See how these Christians love one another!' is as good as a subtitle. In the case of paedophile priests, we do not see media exploration of the spiritual and religious dimension of the tragedy. We see traumatized adults, often in their bitterness and pain, and we see lawsuits and allegations about bishops who are said to have protected or hidden the guilty men. But it is an incomplete picture. There is almost no analysis of how abuse can occur among people who are, or are assumed to be, spiritually minded, and how it has affected or perhaps destroyed the spirituality of the victims and their contemporaries.

The defining complex of events known as '9/11' that brought into being the twenty-first century is simultaneously presented as wickedness akin to genocide, and as a religiously inspired series of events. There is another subliminal text: look what harm religion can do. This is different from the dilemma posed by a forgotten predecessor that one might call '1/11' in British English calendar abbreviation, '11/1' in American English. On 1 November 1755 at midday, an earthquake in Lisbon killed 30,000 people, many of whom were in church at the time for All Saints Day mass. The intellectual tremors from that event, undermining Christian and deist belief, were far more severe than those from '9/11'. In 1755 the question raised by Voltaire and other commentators was: what sort of God kills, or allows to be killed, thousands of people who are in the act of worshipping him? The ripples from that stone in the pond may still be spreading.

If media reporting can be negative, it can also damage by silence. All reporting is by nature selective. Religion can be damaged by omission, creating the impression that it is not important simply by not mentioning it. Thus the role of the churches, especially Baptist churches, in the downfall of the old Soviet bloc was largely ignored in western reporting. It is noteworthy that three of my four letters to the editors of national newspapers (Right, Centre and Left politically) asking for a statement and discussion of their policies on reporting religious issues remain unanswered. Alan Rusbridger, the one editor to reply, explained that the *Guardian* attempted to be 'neutral in its policy' towards religion and indicated that the paper's journalists represented a wide personal spectrum of views on religions. He conceded that the international aspects of religions were perhaps under-presented in the paper.

The media has also been used as a pulpit for secularists, even though they are unrepresentative of 'the people' if the media is ever supposed to be democratic. A number of vocal secularists work in media jobs. They might fairly be styled 'evangelical atheists'. Some are journalist members of the National Secular Society and use their columns as pulpits of a sort. The National Secular Society (NSS), founded in 1866 by Charles Bradlaugh, is a good example of evangelical secularism. A visit to its web site reveals that its declared aims as 'the national campaigning arm of the secularist movement' are to keep a high public profile, to monitor relevant parliamentary business closely, and to lobby extensively. It puts in the 'shop window' its high-profile associates, who include Richard Dawkins, Ludovic Kennedy, Harold Pinter, Polly Toynbee, Gore Vidal and several MPs, some of whom also appear in the British Humanist Association's web site 'shop window'. The NSS declares that 'secularists believe religion is a private matter . . . and should not be permitted to retain any special privileges'. It aims to scrap the blasphemy laws, to remove taxation privileges for religious bodies, to abolish faith schools, disestablish the Church of England, separate the Crown from religion and set a fixed date for Easter. (This latter is also an interesting commentary on how religion and atheism in England are both dominated by the English worldview. Will the world really change to a fixed date for Easter to accommodate England's atheists, even if they can persuade England's legislators? How great is the influence of the National Secular Society?)

The NSS 'asserts that supernaturalism is based on ignorance and it assails it as the historic enemy of progress'. In other words, by its own faith statement, the NSS is not really relegating religion to the private. It wants to wipe it out altogether. On its web site Peter Atkins claims that 'religion is the institutionalization of prejudice'. So now we know – and what an interesting example of prejudice is provided in that statement. Current targets are therefore Christian 'privilege' and global Islam, especially by virtue of its treatment of women. The web site adds that 'secularists believe that religious schools result in increased levels of sectarianism'. At least this is admitted as a belief, since no research evidence exists to support it on the UK mainland.

Another organization of evangelical atheists who have realized that the media is the marketplace of the present day is the Rationalist Press Association. It too offers personal membership, as well as publishing works of humanism, rationalism and secularism. Together their members are ready to fire letters off to newspapers if religion seems to be gaining ascendancy or uncritically favourable publicity. The British Humanist Association (BHA) is more conciliatory. It works with local Standing Advisory Councils for RE, despite the injustice of a Tory government ruling that its members cannot sit formally on them. It does not wish to abolish RE, but rather that RE should be 'impartial, fair and balanced . . . and that there should be no need for the right to withdraw children from RE'. It wishes to see school collective worship transformed into shared-values assemblies. Its web site concentrates rather more on positive support for humanism than negative attacks on religion, in contrast to the NSS. The BHA provides advice about humanist rites of passage such as funerals and a list of people recognized to conduct them. Like the NSS, it opposes faith schools as divisive.

How much influence do groups like these two have? Coyly, the NSS does not reveal its own membership numbers. One large local evangelical Christian church would probably contain more members, but one would never guess that from the relative media publicity each organization might receive. Davie alleges in *Religion in Britain Since 1945: Believing Without Belonging* (1994) that the influence of these groups extends well beyond their membership numbers. With an apparently continuously receding Christian presence to debate the issues and challenge their views, perhaps that influence will increase. Instead of the inane captions on notice boards outside some churches (e.g. 'What is missing from the Ch - - ch? UR!'), it is newspaper articles that constitute the real 'wayside pulpit' of the twenty-first century. Their writers can attempt to woo virtual passers-by over to their side.

While secularists are busy lambasting religion from the privilege of their media pulpits, there is also the question of the influence of media fiction, particularly comedy. Are comedy programmes harmless fun, or might they have a deleterious effect on perceptions of religion? *The Vicar of Dibley* starred Dawn French in several series depicting the trials of a young woman vicar arriving in a traditional parish, facing strong opposition from a middle-aged, right-wing, male churchwarden who is gradually won over. This may have been forward-looking in its day and supportive of the then recent change in the Church of England to allow women priests. Unfortunately for the media image of Christianity, the Dibley church council comprised dimwits, buffoons and at least one character in whom a strong hint of perversion lurked under the surface. *Father Ted*, screened in the UK, the USA and Ireland, is a Roman Catholic priest banished by his bishop for 'financial irregularities' and associated with Father Jack, a thinly disguised alcoholic, all in the best laughable taste. In *Dad's Army* (first broadcast in 1968, gaining audiences up to ten million and attracting two generations of viewers), Frank Williams played the Reverend Timothy Farthing, the vicar of St Aldhelm's, Walmington-on-Sea, an unmasculine, pretentious man with a high-pitched voice, fastidious about church affairs and standing on his dignity. He is supported and hindered by his officious verger, Mr Yeatman (Edward Sinclair), clad in cassock and flat cap. Williams, who played the part extremely well, was actually a committed Anglo-Catholic, a lay member of the General Synod of the Church of England and the Crown Appointments Commission. He wrote that Farthing, although usually harmless, was not 'a terribly good advert for the Church'[45] but went on:

> I really do not think that clergymen can be treated as an endangered species who can only be shown in a good light.

In media fiction on the whole, religion is very clearly depicted as the preoccupation largely of the middle-aged and elderly and of buffoons, fools or occasionally rogues. We do not see much spirituality. In this sense it is a legitimate development of the tradition established by George Eliot in *Scenes of Clerical Life* (1857). Eliot's clergy in these vignettes are, for their time, shockingly ordinary except for the evangelical curate Edgar Tryan. Even he dies from consumption made worse by overwork and bad accommodation. The Reverend Amos Barton is sustained by human kindness rather than religious faith in his time of need. The Church is a bad employer. Faith is a threadbare, rather second-hand affair. Mr Gilfil's story has as its only redeeming feature human love, which is powerless to save. Although fictitious, these scenes marked the end of the placing of the clergy on a pedestal. Eliot's humanistic conclusion is that only good works live on.

The cinema's depiction of religion must be presumed to influence audiences, although again it is not easy to say precisely how. The figure of Jesus remains an enduringly fascinating one for film directors. Pasolini's *The Gospel According to St Matthew* (1966), Ray's *King of Kings* (1961), Stevens' *The Greatest Story Ever Told* (1965), belong to a long tradition of screen depictions of Jesus. *The Last Temptation of Christ* (1988, MCA-Universal), directed by Martin Scorsese and adapted from Nikos Kazantzakis' 1960 novel, containing a scene in which Jesus is shown making love to Mary Magdalene, is about Satan's offer to save Jesus from the cross and establish him as a comfortable family man. The cinematic tradition includes music as well, with *Jesus Christ Superstar* and *Godspell* (in both cases the stage show appeared in 1971, the film in 1973). Superstar is a courageous man, who dies for his beliefs. In the stage show the crucifixion is the end. There is not even a hint of resurrection. It is in the best atheistic tradition. *Godspell*, billed as 'the Gospel for today', is a version of the life of Christ, 'the Chief Clown', told by ten clowns. It claims to be based on Matthew's gospel and the concept of the Clown-Christ as developed by Harvey Cox, Professor of Divinity at Harvard. Integral to the show is urban blight and poverty: the film is set in New York City. In 2000 animation entered the line of film lives of Jesus with Hayes' *The Miracle Maker*.

Another controversial portrait of Jesus was produced in 2004. Mel Gibson's *The Passion of the Christ* was based on the last 12 hours of Jesus' life, employing 'flashbacks' and Aramaic dialogue. There was argument over the graphic violence and whether, for instance, a 25-minute scourging scene was justified. Like all films about Jesus, it is essentially the gospel according to the director. Many Jesus films are in the tradition of the apocryphal gospels, fantasy and conjecture, filling in the gaps in the story of Jesus told in the canonical gospels. There is also a long cinematic tradition based on the desire to shock, which applies to film treatments of the Jesus story. How critically such films are viewed by their audiences is unclear. But they are good for the box office.

The process of secularization continues relentlessly

A Muslim commentator could say in 1990 that 'Christianity has faced the cold and riddling gaze of secular modernity for almost two centuries'.[46] He argues that a living religion becomes ossified if it isolates itself from the scientific and cultural influences that give structure to the lives of ordinary believers. Christianity has historically maintained a distinction between the sacred and the profane, the religious and the secular, from apostolic times when the gospel was first taken to the Greeks. Despite Aquinas and Augustine, the tension has always remained. But, fuelled by the Enlightenment, reason and rationalism have come to dominate.

> Christianity is at root only relevant to men's basic and unalterable condition – a condition of sin and estrangement. If it does not offer a remedy for our fundamental ailments, its own distinctive voice will be drowned out by louder voices and alternative confidences.[47]

Chadwick notes that a liberal state, which will want to treat all religions even-handedly, will become increasingly secular itself as it does this.[48] T. Luckman sees the characteristics of modern society as the autonomy of humankind, self-expression, self-realization, the mobility ethos, the emancipation of sexuality and the family – but a rewritten family operating as the cradle for individual autonomy.[49] Luckman's characteristics do not sit easily with traditional religious beliefs and values and their dominance in our society may be linked to religion's decline. Coping with old age and death is not among them. These are both issues society still does not readily face. The hospice movement has to be credited for providing excellent palliative care for the terminally ill and relief for their carers, but in-patient treatment has removed death from the everyday and ordinary, from the home, and placed it out of view. Similarly, it is hard for the nuclear family, with both parents at work and perhaps noisy teenagers, to cope with nursing Gran in their home, but there is still a sense that when they are consigned to care homes, we are putting the fragile elderly in the waiting room for death. Out of sight, out of mind? We can therefore get on with a secular lifestyle, which assumes by its emphasis on the busy-ness of today that we shall live for ever. We deceive ourselves if we think that 'old' is merely a state of mind that can be overcome by an effort of the will or a mountain bike. Religions, in contrast, tend to affirm a view of life which takes ageing and death into account and faces the one certain fact we each hold about the future: one day we shall die. Are we as a society ready to hear this?

If lifestyle of this sort carries a set of implicitly secular assumptions, the most obvious evidence of relentless secularization consists in the continuing disappearance of the Christian landscape. One example of this is Mothering Sunday, observed on the fourth Sunday of Lent. It was known sometimes as Refreshment Sunday, because its allowed a day's break in the Lent fast and included special treats such as simnel cake, a fruit cake with two layers of almond paste and topped with eleven marzipan balls (the disciples minus Judas). People would go to their own mother church, perhaps the cathedral, to give thanks for the role of Mother Church herself or the Virgin Mary, 'Mother of God', in their lives. The custom later arose of giving a small gift to one's own mother as a token of appreciation on this day. Gradually the day itself was transformed into Mother's Day, a secular time to send a card and present to Mum. The greetings-card industry soon invented an entirely secular parallel, Father's Day, in mid-June, a hitherto low time of year for greetings-card sales. In the USA, Mother's Day was always about one's own 'mom', having arisen in Philadelphia and West Virginia from the grief of Anna Reese Jarvis at the death of her mother. In 1914 Congress established it as the second Sunday in May.

Hallowe'en, All Hallows Eve, itself replacing the earlier pre-Christian festival of Samhain which marked the summer's end, has completely disappeared from the Christian landscape. All Saints Day (1 November) commemorates all the Christian saints, known and unknown. All Souls Day (2 November) remembers the 'souls of the faithful departed'. Hallowe'en (31 October) was once a time of preparation, when the supernatural was held to prevail, when spirits of the dead might be on the move, when interest in divination was rife. (One might wonder in passing how Christian this actually was. It was certainly never a high-profile Christian event.) However, in the mid-1960s, in towns near a US Air Force base, such as Huntingdon, American children brought into the UK their tradition of 'trick or treating'. It did not gain ground until the late 1980s, when the manufacturers realized that in cards, costumes and 'candies', there was a lot of money to be made in a pre-Christmas spend. When small children went from door to door in their immediate neighbourhood, often accompanied by an older sibling or parent, it was innocent enough. But trick-or-treating became an excuse, like Christmas carolling, for doorstep begging and at worst for nasty-minded children to commit cruel pranks, damaging property and frightening elderly people living alone. 'Mischief Night' is a generous misnomer; 'Nasties' Night' would be more apt in some localities. It now seems out of control in some places, except that a curious balance has crept in resulting from the national fear of paedophilia, which prevents some children from appearing on doorsteps to demand goodies from potential murderers lurking inside the house.

Christmas has become increasingly secular. It currently lasts from September until the end of January. Even some churches have largely abandoned Advent as a season with its own hymns and carols, since everyone else is singing Christmas songs from late September. In the USA decorations are often taken down on Boxing Day, as people are fed up with it all by then. Ignored is the Feast of Stephen (26 December), formerly a timely reminder that Christian belief can be costly as well as cosy (Acts 6.8—8.1), to be replaced by the Christmas sales – the Festival or Feast of Consumerism. Stephen was stoned by a mob. But the people stoned now at Christmas are senselessly drunk. The ritual of carolling on the doorstep is reduced now to an abbreviated commercial enterprise. Imperious ringing of the doorbell to bring people away from TV is followed by a hastily rendered verse or simply 'wishing' ('We wish you a merry Christmas' etc.), frequently sung badly and too fast by children who want to collect the money and run. Shops increasingly sell 'season's cards', as if Christmas is unmentionable, and the pictorial images are often of winter or some Dickensian scene, rarely of anything to do with the Christian Christmas. The star of Christmas is not the Star of the East but, of course, 'FC' rather than 'JC', and the dominating motives are presents and alcohol, both in excess. Secularization is often linked to commercialization.

Father Christmas is a curious figure, who corresponds to nearly all the things small children are told about God, if they are told anything at all. Father Christmas lives in a distant place; God lives in rather spooky old buildings called 'the house of God', which are locked to keep him in. You never – or rarely – see Father Christmas or God, though you do meet their helpers. Your parents talk about them in a different, slightly strained voice and seem embarrassed by probing questions. When you press others with your queries, strange glances are exchanged between the adults. There is an air of conspiracy, uncertainty, like when you asked where Grandma had gone and they eventually told you, reluctantly, that she had gone to be with Jesus. Father Christmas can be in different places at the same time. He seems to like department stores, which is understandable as they are full of toys. He can travel magic-fast! He likes children. He gives good things to children, if they are good – the moral clause. Some are still threatened that he 'won't come' if they are naughty. You can make contact with him if you want, by letter or visit, but you are under no obligation. For most of the time you can ignore him. In many ways Father Christmas runs in parallel to God. He *is* God in an accessible, smiling, harmless, yo-ho-ho-ing, domesticated human form, complete with wellies. But when children are deprived of their literal belief in Father Christmas, what does it do to their developing image of God?

The infant's pre-Christmas 'Gimme, gimme, gimme' ('I want, I want, I want') graduates to the adult's spending binge. There is even a hidden rule of equivalence involved in the secular Christmas: people are deeply embarrassed if they have given a present costing a lot less, or a lot more, than the one they have received in return. In other words, we spend on others what we expect them to spend on us. Hijacked by consumerists, Jesus' golden rule has become: 'Spend upon others as you would have them spend upon you.' The shower of presents is a thinly disguised festival of self-indulgence and the day of credit-card reckoning is, like the *parousia*, in the future. Frances Chesterton's carol opens with the words 'How far is it to Bethlehem?' The answer is that it is now a very long way.

City councils in some multifaith cities now decorate city centres in December with 'season's greetings' illuminations and no longer 'Christmas greetings'. This is said to be because to give a Christian greeting might discriminate against members of religions other than Christianity. Politicians don't want to give offence. But offence to whom? None of the non-Christian religious communities has complained, and since Muslims honour Jesus as a prophet – the Qur'an itself teaches the Virgin Birth – the Islamic community is unlikely to be offended about Jesus being remembered. Members of faiths other than Christianity are always glad to see or to join in their counterparts' celebrations; even atheists do not sit tight-lipped, refusing to sing Christmas carols. Once again, unthinking secularist approaches seem to be in the ascendancy.

For many years, a tutor in a university (not my own) used in the last week of the autumn term to bring a keyboard into the education department where he worked. A group of students would join him in the foyer to sing Christmas songs and carols and collect for charity. Hundreds of pounds were raised. It was also fun. But in 2003 there came a decree from an internal magnate in the department. The tutor was told that he could no longer do this, because the university is 'secular' and no celebration of a religious nature should be permitted in any open public space. It would have to move to a seminar room, so as not to force the possibly unwelcome theme on those passing innocently through the foyer. By what right did the potentate censor religion – as it happens, the major religion of that place and the UK – in a free country? What secular value has been put in its place? If the universities permit behaviour like this, what hope is there for less intelligent human groupings?

The real solution, of course, is to honour all religions and put up lights for Eid, Guru Nanak's birthday, Divali, Hanukah, etc. But instead, a prowling secularism seems to be gaining ground. In British culture, if Muslims want public influence it is apparently unacceptable; but when minority secularists want it, it is somehow acceptable. Secularist public partying is OK; religious public partying is apparently not. If religions are off the streets, invisible, we are *de facto* coercing passers-by into unbelief. There is some danger that the UK is heading towards a situation like that in the USA and France, in which an almost paranoid desire to separate church and state prevails. At Christmas 2003 various businesses and churches in Virginia, USA, were criticized for displaying a manger scene in public. In 2004 a US high school (pupil ages 14–18) banned from a school notice board a flyer promoting a voluntary Christian fellowship club. On the same board were flyers that promoted a new club for homosexuals. This was officially permitted. How 'free' is the USA?

Of course, all this is not to suggest that Christmas has become totally secular. Infant-school nativity plays still present a sentimental and often unbiblical version of the birth of Jesus, while overcome mums mop their eyes and members of the cast bedecked in dressing gowns and towels sheepishly wave to Gran in the audience. Christmas Eve mass is still often packed to standing. Christingle services have proved a popular import from Moravian Christianity. The proclamation of a loving God, appearing in person as a vulnerable baby, is still made. Some British shop windows display crib scenes. The story is perennial. But is it viewed as just a story? Can Christmas break out of the consumer wrappings we have tied it in?

For the churches this constitutes a serious crisis, of which they may be only dimly aware. Stridently to condemn what British society has produced in the name of Christmas will simply cast the churches in an anti-fun, negative, puritanical role in wider society – a latter-day Scrooge. They would probably be derided by the media and certainly ignored by the public. Something as complex, appealing to consumers and commercially manipulated as the modern British Christmas will not be tamed by a piece of social and theological analysis, however accurate. On the other hand, going along with things as they are submerges the basic Christian proclamation. This claims that lives are changed by love more than by possessions. It asserts that the pursuit of pleasure is not the highest goal of humankind, that God is on the side of the poor and the oppressed rather than the present-laden, that God is in our midst in unexpected ways and places. Luke states this unequivocally, right in the middle of his narrative of the birth of Jesus (1.46–55). It is a crisis for the churches because opposing what Christmas has become and the alternative, endorsing it, both have big problems – but who will listen anyway?

The word 'culture' connects with the Latin *cultura* and carries a root meaning to grow, to take care of, to cultivate. What does our culture grow, take care of, cultivate? Apparently not religion. Fore argues that 'the primary task of the church is to make it possible for the Gospel to be heard in our time'.[50] One could say similar things about some other world religions, the missionary ones. They have to make it possible for their truth to be heard in the time and society in which they find themselves. In order to do this it is necessary to understand the host culture and enter into dialogue with it. 'Religion comes clothed in culture's language, uses culture's history and its art forms, relies on those common understandings which are supplied by culture's current mythology, and refers to current cultural experiences'.[51] Our culture is weighted against traditional Christianity, the Christianity of the churches. It represents a rejection of the spiritual source that has brought the culture into existence.

The synoptic Gospels contain the narrative of the rejection of Jesus at Nazareth by his own people (Mark 6.1–6; Matthew 13.53–58; Luke 4.16–30). Each writer gives the narrative a particular focus. For Mark, Jesus could do no mighty work in Nazareth, except to lay his hands on a few sick people and heal them (verse 5). He was amazed at their unbelief. For Matthew he would not do mighty works there because of their unbelief, i.e. he chose not to (verse 58). Luke focuses on Jesus' preaching in the synagogue, which culminates in attempted murder or execution by stoning (verse 29), but he also implies that Jesus did little or no healing work in Nazareth (verse 23). A superficial reading of Mark might suggest that in order to heal, Jesus required faith on the part of the sick people themselves. Elsewhere Mark rebuts this (2.5), just as he relates that it was the faith of the paralysed man's friends, or Jairus (5.23) or the Syro-phoenician woman (7.28), not the personal faith of the patient that was important. But what the Gospels clearly present is a climate of unbelief. In such a climate perhaps Mark is right that Jesus *could* do no great work, while Matthew's *would* do no mighty work is an attempt to protect Jesus' power. This incident from two millennia ago raises the question for us of how much is possible in a climate of unbelief. Religion in Britain is certainly under pressure from fashion, from deliberate attack, from media image, from secularization. It is not easy for those growing up in this culture to hear the claims of institutional Christianity, or other institutional religions, in a way that does them justice. But despite this choking culture and the continuing downward line on the graph, religion has by no means disappeared, as we shall discover. If Christianity grew out of almost nothing in a climate of unbelief, it, or another religion, can do it again – even in England.

3

'I've Got a Dog Now': The Death and Life of Christianity after 1945

I used to go to church every week, but not any more, because I've got a dog now . . .

(Year 6 pupil number 74, aged 11, from the University of Exeter Biblos survey, 2003)

The collapse of institutional Christianity in the UK after 1945

It has become almost a convention to refer to British – and European – culture as post-Christian. Indeed for Don Cupitt, history itself has ended, as we no longer have our former belief in progress or in linear, eschatological time.[1] We control the past and can rewrite it at whim. The idea of a better future has evaporated. In his essay 'Post-Christianity', Cupitt can offer only a belief in *anatta*, the Buddhist no-self doctrine, and in the Abrahamic prohibition on idolatry. Death is the final end. Another philosopher, V. Pratt, finds his only comfort in the myth of Sisyphus, who was condemned forever to push a large boulder to the top of a hill, only to have it roll to the bottom and have to start again.[2] Is Sisyphus the icon of a post-Christian time, he ponders, in which personal existence loses its meaning? This case might be strengthened in postmodern discourse since Pratt wrote. Pratt, adopting Camus before him, suggests that Sisyphus' act draws meaning from within. Sisyphus derives enjoyment from the physical effort itself. Thus the act for him becomes intrinsically worthwhile. Is this all we are left with in a post-Christian society, to make the best of it and grin grimly in the gloom?

But 'post-Christian' is a value-laden term, which does not do justice to the complexity of religious belief or to the 71.6 per cent of the

UK population who identified themselves as Christian in the 2001 national census. The more one scrutinizes the term, the more difficult it is to defend as an example of the sort of finality of which Don Cupitt and Callum Brown so confidently speak. Christmas, Easter and harvest services can still fill many churches. There is still a demand for Christian rites of passage, even though civic alternatives are now gaining ground. Many more people buy their parish magazine and contribute to the church roof repair fund than attend the services. If this is residual Christianity, it is a large residue. As Wolffe rightly cautions, this does not necessarily imply explicit personal acceptance of Christianity on the part of those involved. But it can legitimately be seen as 'a reflection of tradition, community loyalties and a desire to mark the key events' of both the annual and the personal life cycle.[3] Emphasizing the superiority of personal acceptance of religion over these other features is a very Protestant way of critiquing religious conviction, however. It is very evangelically Protestant to want to know if you have accepted Jesus into your life and when. Many Christians get on with Christian living without this sort of preoccupation or declaration. Challenged, those 'believers' who constitute 'residual Christianity' would strongly assert their Christian identity. By what authority do we unseat them?

David Jenkins criticizes the term 'post-Christian' sharply on the theological and linguistic grounds that it presupposes a Christian era before it, which is 'historical nonsense and biblical blasphemy . . . In fact there never has been a Christian age.' The only possible Christian age lies ahead when the Kingdom of God fully and finally comes. To identify a period in history as a 'Christian age' is to treat Christianity merely as a cultural phenomenon, Jenkins argues, and in such a time people might not have real faith in God but instead be conforming to a cultural habit or historic fashion.[4] However, the idea of a Christian era was made plausible by the historical fact that for many years the church was one of the major 'powers that be'. Jenkins applies the label 'Christendom' to this period, so he refers to the present time by the term 'post-Christendom', meaning that the hegemony of the church is over and that western civilization and culture do not take God or Christianity for granted. 'The world does not help us to believe in God, nor do we strengthen our faith by conformity.'[5] Clearly, in the light of Jenkins' theological and historical critique of 'post-Christian' and the sociological evidence of a large residue of Christianity, one has to conclude that 'post-Christian' as a descriptor is premature, simplistic, open to challenge and misleading. 'Post-Christendom' or 'post-ecclesiastical' would be more accurate phrases. Unfortunately, however, 'post-Christian' has caught on. It is frequently used uncritically and perhaps helps to create an image of Christianity that makes it look more dead than it is.

What an attack on the term 'post-Christian' cannot do, however, is to disguise the fact that Christian religiosity, in the sense in which sociologists of religion use the term, is in recession. As we have seen, church congregations have declined significantly. This decline accelerated from the 1960s onwards, especially among nonconformity. Methodist numbers haemorrhaged for the entire twentieth century. The United Reformed Church, formed in 1972 by a merger of many English Congregational churches with the Presbyterian Church of England, could not halt decline from its inception onwards. Even Roman Catholicism, with its once strict discipline of attendance at mass that Protestants both admired and resented, has witnessed decline.

In 1998 a questionnaire was sent to every Trinitarian church in England on behalf of the English Church Attendance Survey. It was a survey, not a census, i.e. it asked for average numbers, not a head count on a specified Sunday. The resultant figures suggest that the steep decline in attendance of the 1980s had continued into the 1990s, and also that those attending church attended less frequently than they used to. This was the proverbial double whammy. The 12 per cent who went to church weekly in 1979 had fallen to 7.5 per cent by 1998. This represented 3.5 million out of a 50 million population. Another 2.7 per cent attend once or twice per month and a further 6 per cent less frequently. If their members all attended less frequently than once a month, it would give the churches the social cohesion and spiritual force of a café. The survey also revealed a move away from Sunday worship towards midweek worship, which might reflect different patterns of work and leisure: 2.4 per cent of the population attend for midweek but not Sunday worship. Such services are available in 42 per cent of churches, the average congregation numbering 21. Only 14 per cent of churches have a youth worship service – average attendance 43.

Songs of Praise, a hymn-singing programme with interviews cut in, is watched by 1.9 per cent of the population. Its largest single audience was 11.4 million at Christmas 1988, but most of these viewers do not attend church. Half the *Songs of Praise* viewers are over the age of 65. No doubt this will lead to long-term re-scheduling to an off-peak time such as 1 a.m., which will at least please the insomniac elderly. In 1998 0.4 per cent of the population was attending an Alpha Course. The churches were estimated to be losing 1,000 children (under 15s) per week and to be showing a slant towards the upper (65+) age group, most particularly in Methodism. One Methodist church in six can expect to close by 2010. There are no teenagers aged 15 to 18 in the congregations of 52 per cent of churches. Evangelicals have declined at only 10 per cent of the rate of non-evangelicals. The evangelical mainstream has grown while numbers of broad evangelicals (those accepting modern biblical scholarship) and charismatic evangelicals have both declined. One person in eight attending church is non-white, double the figure in the general population. In terms of attendance, but not the number of congregations, Roman Catholicism is the biggest English denomination within the mainstream institutional churches, but its numbers are also in decline.

There are 16,000 churches in England with a regular Sunday congregation of 50 or fewer and 3,000 churches with a congregation of 300 or more (2,000 of them Roman Catholic). In the late 1990s fewer new churches were being started than in the late 1980s. Seven thousand church buildings dating from prior to 1300 are still in use; 33 per cent of church buildings are 'listed'. However, only 33 per cent of churches responded to this questionnaire, the main stated reason for non-compliance being lack of time, so care has to be taken with generalizations based on this research.[6] Brierley reads a clear message in these statistics, that 'if present trends continue, we could literally be one generation from extinction'.[7] Davie, on the other hand, wonders whether the process of decline is partly because the Church of England and its historic offshoot, Methodism, are less historically linked to the mainstream European churches than the Roman Catholic Church and Reformed churches such as the Church of Scotland. This might account for their greater decline in a strengthening Europe.[8] By 2004 the claim was made in the media that 930,000 Muslims attend a place of worship at least once per week compared to 916,000 Anglicans.

Audiences for UK religious programmes on radio and TV seem to be declining. A ten-fold increase in BBC output over a decade was accompanied by a fall of one-third of programmes with religious topics, which currently account for 550 hours on national radio and TV. ITV carries 104 hours, which its programme director wanted to off-load to the BBC or Channel 4.[9] Of course, it is not just the number of hours that matter, but the quality of the broadcasts and the timing of transmission. Despite attempts by some programme chiefs to drop it, 'Thought for the Day' on the high-prestige Radio 4 *Today* programme, runs at peak time Monday to Saturday at around 7.45 a.m. It is the successor to 'Lift up your hearts' and 'Ten to Eight', together dating back to 1939. In 1986 and again in 1990, audience research showed it to be more popular than the sport or business slots in *Today*. It has a range of speakers, reflecting on a news item from a religious point of view. The most popular speaker for years was Reform Rabbi Lionel Blue, who himself commented that 'it forces you to make your religion relevant to daily life'.[10] Research in 1994 confirmed the item's continuing popularity, but also revealed that 20 per cent of listeners did not like it.[11] A controversial piece can still elicit up to 1,000 letters, emails and phone calls. Many listeners protested when seven seasoned male Christian speakers were 'rested' in 1996 to be replaced by more women and people from other faiths.

C. S. Prebish notes that in the 1970s in the USA, the churches were more flexible and began to adjust their service times to fit major sporting events and TV programmes.[12] This entailed accepting that at one level they too were a leisure activity in a competitive situation. Billy Graham spoke up in favour of sport as a suitable activity for Christians, keeping them busy with healthy pursuits. In the USA many winners thank God and their 'mom' for their achievements in prize-winning speeches. In the American university, the enormous status of sport was something their churches and chaplaincies could not ignore. Prebish argues that religion and sport each have a body of beliefs, accepted in faith by large numbers of people. In both the tradition is maintained essentially by men. Sport has saints and ruling patriarchs, high councils and scribes who report it. Like religion, sport has shrines – Halls of Fame and the like – and emotive symbols. Both sport and religion are the subject of merchandising. They use a common language of dedication, sacrifice and commitment. The social euphoria of the game promotes a festive communion. Prebish might have added that both sport and religion impose a discipline and claim to lead, among other things, to self-discovery. Prebish reaches the conclusion that '*sport is religion* [his italics] for growing numbers of Americans',[13] but he does not argue that all sport is religion. Another example of the idea of religion as a leisure activity with an appropriate metaphor comes from the former East Germany. Here, working with kindergarten children usually from an atheistic back-ground, Anna-Katharina Szagun of the University of Rostock tried to identify their concepts of God, by means of enabling them to produce models and drawings to illustrate their thoughts. One child modelled a fitness studio and was able to explain that an encounter with God would be like a visit to such a place: a toning-up process in which you discover things about yourself.

The British Sunday school is a relatively neglected area for research, yet in 1850 two million working-class children were enrolled under 250,000 working-class teachers. As late as 1950 roughly 50 per cent of British children attended Sunday schools. Nowadays it is hard to produce a comparative figure, as some Sunday schools have been subsumed into integrated family worship and many have changed their name. But it is perhaps no more than 5 per cent. Even in the 1950s, to be sent to Sunday school was cissy for boys, something one tried hard to hide from one's non-attending peers. As the twentieth century advanced, Sunday schools began to look less and less sophisticated in a society that was embracing a whole range of increasingly sophisticated gadgets, hobbies and lifestyles. Moreover, largely unnoticed by the churches, they had by then lost their principal function, the provision of secular education. From the point of view of indoctrination, the big question is whether Sunday schools indoctrinated children into the Christian faith, or out of it. On the surface, church attendance statistics would suggest that on the whole, the experience of Sunday school was unattractive. It was an inoculation against institutional Christianity rather than in favour of it. But Sunday schools probably account for some of the 71.6 per cent who state their Christian adherence in the 2001 reli-gious census.

The Sunday school has a long history, stretching back to around 1780 and the work of Robert Raikes in Gloucester and Hannah More in the Mendip region of Somerset, but its nature has changed radi-cally over those 225 years. Sunday schools were founded originally to teach the children of the poor to read (the Bible) and to do limited basic writing, since 'day school' education was neither universal nor free before 1870. Their sister agencies, the ragged schools – an amazing proclamation of social class in their very name – coexisted to teach the four 'R's' (reading, writing, arithmetic and religion) up to the 1870s. Sunday schools had purpose as part of the Church's philanthropic provision and also reflected its historic role as a provider of education. There were morning and afternoon sessions – not evenings, as oil lighting or candles were the only options in the early Sunday school era. Each session might last up to three hours. Three to five hours of instruction per week in small classes, which were graded by ability, using specialist texts, was a significant factor in the rise of mass literacy. The Victorian graduates of these classes included those who were to become the foremen and managers of industry. Children also frequently owed their holidays to Sunday schools. After the arrival of railways and until the Second World War, the Sunday school trip, often a charter train to the seaside for the day, shared between different churches and chapels in a town or city, was the working-class child's only holiday.

Surprisingly, there was no strong tradition of viewing the purpose of the Sunday school as intrinsically the teaching of the young members, or members-to-be, of the Church. Sunday schools remained preoccupied with 'teaching' rather than nurturing. The one big point of contact with the host church in nonconformity was the Sunday school anniversary. This was a major annual event in the nonconformist church year, often with three services and sometimes spread over two Sundays. The children sat on specially constructed tiered platforms in the chapel and performed hymns, recitations and readings as part of a service featuring a guest preacher and often an orchestra rather than just the organ. Admiring families and visitors from other congregations filled the chapel. The girls wore white dresses, the boys wore white shirts and little suits. It was a big event, like the annual Whitsuntide outdoor processions of the north of England, with their brass bands and banners and hymn singing at points along the route. But did the months of rehearsals justify the event? And did the children enjoy it? Sunday school anniversaries faded as the platforms annually became emptier from the 1960s onwards. Only a few survive.

Another associated problem was that some Sunday schools

became largely divorced from their host church, except that the adult staff worshipped there – sometimes. In some churches the main Sunday school session was held in the afternoon, which did not often coincide with adult worship. It was common, therefore, for children to graduate from Sunday school or Anglican confirmation class to non-attendance at church in or before their early teens. So some Sunday schools turned themselves into 'junior church' and tried to integrate their children into part of the adult worship. This practice is now common in the remaining Sunday schools, while all-age worship has replaced or complemented it in some churches.

In the 1940s and 1950s it was assumed that the role of the Sunday school and the role of religious instruction in the day school were broadly the same. Each teacher was held to reinforce the work of the other. But with rising standards and resources in the day schools, Sunday schools easily appeared amateur in their teaching and shabby in their premises by comparison. Comparison was inevitable, since many children attended both types of school, whereas few teachers taught in both. The Sunday-school teachers were usually untrained, so success depended on their natural flair, or lack of it, and the standard-issue denominational lesson book. There was a steady haemorrhage of children as they got older. Sometimes young teenage 'teachers' were recruited in an effort to keep them involved. Sometimes ancient 'teachers' continued in the Sunday school long beyond their years of usefulness. Sometimes adults with no desire or particular aptitude to be Sunday-school teachers took classes out of loyalty, because nobody else would volunteer to take them. The whole terminology of 'teachers', 'lessons', 'classes', 'registers', encouraged comparison with day schooling. And in any comparison – the education and training of their teachers, the quality of the resources, the premises – the Sunday school came off worse. (This was not the case in the USA, where, with no religious education in most 'public' schools, the churches became much more professionally oriented in their work with children.)

Moreover, children resented being *sent* by their parents, who remained at home to enjoy a quiet Sunday afternoon with the newspaper or 'wireless', or more secret uninterrupted marital pleasure. In the sabbatarian Britain of the 1950s, many nonconformist children were forbidden to 'play out' on Sunday, so they may well have been bored and in the way indoors.

With long-established universal day-school education, it was over-looked that children might not be desperately keen to go to 'school' on Sunday when they had spent five days there and some evenings on homework already. So it often came about that those children who went on from Sunday school into active adult church member-ship were the survivors of the system rather than its products.

Post-war prosperity had its impact on Sunday schools as else-where. The the arrival of 'charas' (charabancs, motor coaches) trans-ferred the euphoria surrounding the holiday outing to the road. But as children began to holiday in the family car in exotic, distant places, like pre-motorway Torquay or Bournemouth, or even to travel by air to Spain and other foreign destinations, a day trip to a local resort was no longer anything to get excited about.

The increasingly common ownership of cars in the 1960s took families out for a drive in the hitherto unexplored countryside on Sunday afternoons, or to visit relatives who had previously been sev-eral bus rides away. This hastened the collapse of afternoon Sunday schools and their relocation to the morning. The development of Sunday as a leisure and shopping day, the dispersion of family mem-bers far beyond a single town or village and the rise of weekends away continued to bite into the time available for the remaining Sunday schools in the 1990s. It became harder to find adults who were willing to commit time on 50 Sundays to act as leaders or teachers. A rota system became inevitable. This was mirrored in spasmodic attendance by children. They no longer viewed the class or group as a weekly event in their life.

There are notable exceptions. The Metropolitan Tabernacle (Baptist) in London's Elephant and Castle was founded by C. H. Spurgeon. It still claims 700 members in its Sunday school and Bible class, led by 60 staff and meeting on Sunday afternoon. Its minister, Peter Masters, has co-authored a book whose title sums up the church's priority for youth work: *The Necessity of Sunday Schools in this Post-Christian Era*. Many more churches at local level can claim good numbers in their children's groups, whatever name they have now given to these descendants of the work of Robert Raikes. The modern Sunday school or its equivalent is not often atttended by children without their parents. It is more enjoyable than a generation ago. But the mass national attendance has gone.

Another tantalizing and unresearched question is what happened to the beliefs and attitudes of that 50 per cent of children who were in Sunday school in the 1940s and 1950s. Most of them are still alive. We know some things about them. The religious education that they experienced in day school would at that time have been largely biblical. Most of them did not move into adult attendance at church. They did not send their children to Sunday school. Their children show no signs of sending their own children to Sunday school. These children, unlike their grandparents in their young days, can now avail themselves of secular marriage or funeral arrangements in settings that aesthetically compete with churches and in a few that offer bizarre alternatives. They have more of this culture's watchword: choice. And if we return to that ageing 50 per cent of Sunday school 'graduates' of the 1940s and 1950s, they must comprise some of the 71.6 per cent in the 2001 census who described themselves as Christian. They are probably a large proportion of the viewers of *Songs of Praise*. What will their grandchildren fill in on the religious census return when their time comes? Surely that percentage will dip as time passes.

On Saturday 4 June 1921 at 12 noon, some hopeful 11-year-olds from Flintshire county schools sat a general knowledge paper, as part of the examination for entrance scholarships to grammar school. In 50 minutes they had to answer any six out of 20 questions. Candidates therefore had an average time of just over eight minutes per question, excluding time to read the question and check the answer. Question 20 asked:

> Who were the authors of the following hymns: Lead, kindly light; Abide with me; Rock of Ages; From Greenland's icy mountains; Onward, Christian Soldiers; O God, our help in ages past?
> Of the above, write out the hymn you know best.

Today even regular churchgoers would be hard put to answer all parts of that question correctly. This sort of exemplar is from time to time used to bewail the loss of Christian education in church and school. In one sense, that is right. It is part of the process by which signals of Christianity are disappearing from the landscape, along with the year-round availability of hot cross buns (see p. xvi) and a greater religious or more accurately, Christian, illiteracy. But that judgement is hard to make, for three reasons. The first is that we do not know in detail what teaching process the students who chose to

answer this question had passed through. They might have been subjected to heavy doses of rote learning at the expense of understanding in day school or Sunday school that made the exercise unpleasant
or counter-productive. The second is that students today, who do not
know this information, know many things that their 1921 counterparts did not, especially about world religions. The third problem in
using this question as evidence for the 'good old days' of Christian
education is that we do know that the examination was intended to
be difficult and to reduce the candidates to small enough numbers to
fit the number of scholarship places. Marks in the 40 per cent range
were the average on this paper. Cumulatively, all this means that it is
very difficult to compare children in two different periods of time.
Under the microscope very few golden ages appear quite so golden.

What we can be sure about, however, is that the notion of
Christian education for all had collapsed by the mid-1960s, except in
church schools. Even they came under pressure at the time to
emphasize their common ground with rather than their differences
from county schools, now known as community schools. At the
same time, a change of subject name on the school timetable
occurred that was more than cosmetic. Religious instruction (RI) or
divinity (Div) became religious knowledge (RK) and then religious
education (RE), even though the change was not legally enshrined
until 1988. Religious studies (RS) was later favoured as the descriptor for external examinations, after Ninian Smart's influence on phe-
nomenology as an approach to the subject (see p. 113). The message
was clear. Children were no longer being instructed or advised what
to believe but educated to think and choose for themselves.

While all this was happening in education, there was a decline in
what had been assumed to be traditional Christian morality.
Women's skirts got shorter. Men's hair got longer. Drugs were
beginning to be both public and a 'problem'. Credit became easier
with the arrival of Barclaycard (1966), so 'debt', which once carried
a social stigma, became almost universal. The law relaxed somewhat: legalized abortion (1967), legalized homosexuality (1967),
easier divorce and less stringent censorship (1968). Cohabitation as
an alternative to marriage or preparation for it became open rather
than furtive. Sex outside marriage became increasingly acceptable.
Not only was illegitimacy no longer seen as a stigma, it gradually
became politically incorrect to define someone's parentage in this

way. Pop music was establishing great influence and economic power over its devotees. Television was controversial by virtue of satire (*That Was the Week that Was*, 1963) and language (*Till Death Us Do Part*, 1966). Mary Whitehouse started her 'clean up TV' campaign in 1964. In many of the controversies over these changes the churches were seen to be resistant, adopting a role that could easily be portrayed as negative, rather like trying, too late, to put on the brakes on a runaway vehicle. In this more affluent society, which had endured the harsher 1950s and the rationing of war, people did not want the brakes to be put on. Life was increasingly about enjoyment, not conformity. Another commentator before the 1960s were in full swing thought that a deeper shift had occurred:

> It is easy . . . to live today in a world separated from the ultimates . . . At least, it is not difficult to avoid them if one wants – and the temper of the time, as perhaps also the choice of subjects for the curriculum, encourages such an avoidance.[14]

In this time of steep recession for the churches, Roman Catholicism fared better, despite or perhaps because of what to outsiders seems its anti-modern stance. There are two competing theories to account for this. One argues that the anti-modern stance, with its emphasis on church authority and teaching and attempts to undo Vatican II, helped to hold the church together while other churches fell apart. In this scenario, the Roman Catholic Church was the last bastion of traditional values in Europe, with the Pope as the last absolute monarch. The other theory argues that despite the anti-modern stance, pluralism developed, and it was pluralism that enriched and strengthened Catholicism at parish level. In some ways British Roman Catholicism could be said to reflect belonging without believing – believing in the sense of adhering to church hierarchy, authority and doctrine. As Graham Greene put it:

> 'Are you really an RC?', I asked my aunt with interest . . .
> 'Yes, my dear, only I just don't believe in all the things they believe in.'[15]

Greene, himself a convert to Catholicism, wrote that he became convinced 'of the probable existence of something we call God,

though now I dislike the word with all its anthropomorphic associations and prefer Chardin's Noosphere'.[16] In other words, it is easy to
presume that divergence of belief from orthodoxy occurs only among
unchurched Christian adherents, but the 'orthodox' as individuals can
sometimes be far from orthodox in their beliefs. M. P. Hornsby-Smith
conducted research into Roman Catholic pluralism which embraced
practising Catholics and 'dormant Catholics'.[17] People in four
parishes were questioned about their images of God, their beliefs
about heaven, hell and life after death, and about personal prayer. To
the first question (God) there were found to be 12 different categories
of response. To the second there were nine and in the third, four.
These did not relate to whether the person was a practising Catholic
or not. Nor did they relate always to official church teaching. The conclusion from all this was that although to outsiders the Roman
Catholic Church might appear monolithic and monochrome, it is in
fact plural at parish level. Hornsby-Smith did not add that those *bêtes
noires* of Catholicism to the Protestant mind – papal infallibility,
teaching about birth control, the over-exalted status of Mary –
seemed to be cheerfully ignored by many British Catholics, who
turned out to be surprisingly 'Protestant' in their views. If we are surprised by Catholic pluralism, it is perhaps because we have become
accustomed to the Protestant stereotype that Catholics do and believe
what they are told. But we live in a society in which beliefs are
assumed by many to be optional, cognitive, intellectual allegiances in
the attic of the mind, part of the privatization of religion. Hinde
argues that pluralism like this is a sign of vitality, of personal adjust-
ment, of change in the self-system, which is far wider than merely the
cerebral.[18] Later research commissioned by Rosalie Osmond for her
book *Changing Perspectives: Christian Culture and Morals in
England Today* (1993) touched on more evidence relating to Roman
Catholicism: 23 per cent of Catholics saw 'enjoyment' as compatible
with religion, but only 8 per cent of nonconformists did. Perhaps the
legacy of seventeenth-century Puritanism survives in the Protestant
mind. But if religion has become a leisure activity, seeing it as enjoyable might help, quite apart from the fact that the gospel was intended
to be 'good news'.

We may contrast the steep decline of nonconformity and the
smaller slippage of Roman Catholicism with the fortunes of a relatively small and very 'liberal' Christian group, the Religious Society

of Friends (Quakers), in what is now called Britain Yearly Meeting. Sometimes Friends are perceived by outsiders to be spiritual giants. Perhaps this is because onlookers find it hard to contemplate the idea of sitting through a Meeting for Worship based mainly or sometimes entirely on silent waiting. Or perhaps it is because of Quaker philanthropy and relief work or their peace testimony. It is easy for other Christians to define Friends in negatives: they do not have a professional ministry or set services or a church year (despite major concessions at Christmas) or sacraments as the churches understand them. Despite all these differences Quakers are accepted, even admired, as a group with a particular form of Christian witness. Quakers have maintained their membership levels with small losses. They had approximately 18,000 members and 18,000 'attenders' or adherents, albeit with a distinctly ageing profile, for the last quarter of the twentieth century. But was the price of this survival the abandonment or at least the massive reduction of a distinctive Christian witness? British Friends provide an excellent illustration of what happens when liberal Christians are infected by or embrace uncritically the spirit of the age, in this case very much the British age, not the global age.

Friends (Quakers) were brought into being by George Fox (1624-91) along with others including Margaret Fell (Fox), William Penn, Robert Barclay and the neglected James Nayler. As a result of his own experiences, Fox found the teaching and pastoral care of the 'steeple houses' (churches) inadequate and the experience of their 'professors', those who professed religious belief, to be far short of what true Christians should be. After many religious wanderings, Fox heard an inward voice, which told him, 'There is one, even Christ Jesus, that can speak to thy condition.' From then on he was reliant on Christ, 'the Inward Teacher'. Fox felt called to awaken everyone to be led by 'the divine light of Christ' or the 'inward light' which was held to be distinguishable from the 'natural light' of conscience. Fox came to it by direct experience, which he later believed was confirmed by the Bible. He was a Christian radical who came to call people away from human preaching to be obedient to Christ, their inward teacher.

Thus Quaker worship was based not on 'outward forms', set hymns, written prayers, essay-like sermons timed by an hourglass, liturgical rituals, but on a waiting on the pure Spirit, in preparation for which all the human senses were intended to be stilled. True communion was directly and immediately with the Living God and not via the eating of bread and the drinking of wine. True baptism was an inward cleansing, not an outward sprinkling. Friends saw themselves as 'a true church of Christ gathered together by God'. They set out to bring the nation away from the paid 'professors' and into 'the Life', enduring calumny and persecution for their trouble. By their mode of worship, their attitude to 'hat honour', to swearing oaths, to the ministry of women, and to the use of titles, by their peace testimony, their rejection of a professional clergy, and their organization and business meetings, they were radical reformers. Like many before and after, they attempted to recover the 'pure' gospel that they saw as corrupted by the churches. They sought to bring about the 'convincement' (conversion) of Britain by preaching in the streets and churches.

They did spectacularly well at this at first, until the missionary zeal began to run out of steam around 1700 and the Society began to turn in on itself. By mid-Victorian times the Society had become largely middle class and dynastic. They wore drab Quaker grey and retained 'thee' and 'thou' in their speech, archaic by then, as the second person singular had become 'you'. Friends who married out of the Society were disowned. Quakers were known to be serious-minded (or frankly dull) people. But as Victorian Christianity experienced an evangelical upturn, Quakers too adopted an 'orthodox' evangelical position under the leadership of Joseph John Gurney. This phase prevailed until 1895 and a conference in Manchester, influenced by John Wilhelm Rowntree, which embraced modern thinking about the Bible and science. These two phases in Victorian Quaker history illustrate a disturbing and rather uncritical willingness among Friends to adapt to the spirit or fashion of the age, first evangelicalism, then 'modernism'. This was to be repeated in the closing decades of the twentieth century in a major shift whose results would, if such things ever could, raise George Fox from the dead.

By the late twentieth century, the official documents of the Society and the pages of *The Friend*, the weekly Quaker newspaper, had begun to look decidedly less Christian in tone and content. Spoken ministry in Meetings was increasingly secular, sometimes addressing the moral outrage provided by the various warring adventures of western governments or sometimes offering the 'daffodil ministry', as it was nicknamed, based on aesthetic experience perhaps inspired by the flowers on the meeting room's central table. The leaflet handed out to visitors, 'Your first time in a Quaker Meeting?', by its 1996 edition mentions Jesus only once: 'Some [in Meeting for Worship] will thank God for his inexhaustible love shown in Jesus.' Only *some*. Christianity is not mentioned at all. Quaker freedom from creeds seemed to have produced an anarchic situation where Friends, unaware of their own tradition of spiritual discipline and history, began to view the Society as a friendly group who liked to share a time of silence together in which each individual could believe whatever they chose. One said that they saw the Society 'as a kind of club – very much a do-it-yourself religion. Everyone [in 1960] accepted that there was a God: Jesus had existed as an historical figure.'[19] By the 1990s some Friends openly began to disavow the label 'Christian' and some proclaimed that they were not even theists. A few claimed to be 'Hindu Quakers', Buddhist Quakers', 'Non-theist Quakers', etc. Outside commentators wisely began to distinguish 'Christocentric Friends' from 'universalist Friends'. In the plain speaking for which Quakers used to be famous, this was a distinction between Christian Quakers and non-Christian ones. But the concept of a non-Christian Quaker would have made no more sense than a square circle to the Quakers of the previous 300 years of the Society's history. Its founders would have raged against the idea in language that the decorous Quakers of today would view as distinctly 'unQuakerly'.

Friends had always had a universalist strand in their thinking from the early days, well expressed by William Penn (1693). He wrote that 'the humble, meek, merciful, just, pious and devout souls are everywhere of one religion, and when death has taken off the mask they will know one another'.[20] But it was emphatically a *Christian* universalism. What was happening in the Society in the 1980s and 1990s was different. It was more than universalism. It was the letting go of Christianity. Christians in other churches who got to know about this were – and are – confused. Are Quakers Christian or not? Yes or no? What do Quakers believe? A telephone call to the Friends House enquiry desk in London's Euston Road produces no simple answer to what appears to the enquirer to be a very simple question. The reality in the UK is that Jehovah's Witnesses currently have more declared beliefs in common with the mainstream churches than many Friends.

Some Friends tried to paper the cracks by reiterating their time-honoured formula that words are inadequate for ultimate realities, that Friends can be united in Meeting for Worship, that the light is in all people (but what or whose light?). Some felt that these are divisions of emphasis that do not, ultimately, matter. In the deep silence words are transcended, but in the world we have to use them. Some meetings at local level remain deeply centred, very spiritual and strongly united on Christ, 'the inward teacher'. Ginger groups sprang up to lobby their case within the wider Society: the Seekers, the Quaker Universalist Group (both pro-universalist), the Christian Quaker Renewal Fellowship and the New Foundation Fellowship (both pro-Christian). But in any critical analysis, the Religious Society of Friends began to look increasingly like the famous Polo mint. There was a hole in the middle.

Christian Faith and Practice, the spiritual anthology of the Society, was renamed *Quaker Faith and Practice* in its 1994 version. The 'Advices and Queries', a mixture of spiritual witness and probing questions addressed to individual Friends and their Meetings, were also changed. The 1968 series states unequivocally that 'the love of God draws us to him, a redemptive love shown forth by Jesus Christ in his life and on the cross. He is the Way, the Truth and the Life. As his disciples, we are called to live in the life and power of the Holy Spirit.' Friends are referred to as 'members of the world-wide church of Christ'. The 1994 'Advices' state more vaguely that the Society 'is rooted in Christianity' and 'has always found inspiration in the life and teachings of Jesus'. A phrase about the 'mystery and truth of resurrection' was omitted under odd circumstances at the final meeting to endorse revision. This omission was not in what Friends call 'right ordering'.[21] But it went through. Friends are still advised to 'bring the whole of your life under the ordering of the spirit of Christ' but this is not explicitly related to the Jew Jesus of Nazareth. In other words, 'Christ' is looking suspiciously like an idea or ideal not related to a person in space and time, the inseparable Jesus Christ of Christian proclamation.

This is classic nineteenth-century Liberal Protestant reductionism at work again. Jesus, if significant at all, is essentially a moral teacher, not even a *Jewish* moral teacher. The proclamation that the

Power of God raised him from the dead is notably absent. Heron notes that this move away from the Christian base had taken a mere 30 years.[22] Friends seemed unaware that a similar move had occurred in English Unitarianism a century earlier, with disastrous consequences. That denomination in England was severely weakened, even in its traditional Manchester and London strongholds. The Unitarian and Free Christian Churches via their 2001 General Assembly state that they exist 'to promote a free and inquiring religion through the worship of God and the celebration of life . . . and the upholding of the liberal Christian tradition'. Are they clearer than Friends?

A religious society that disavows creeds, is courageously prepared to engage in dialogue and to seek truth wherever it may be found, will always be liable to be infected by the spirit of the age. As W. R. Inge famously remarked, those who are married to the spirit of the age may find themselves suddenly widowed. It is hard to escape the conclusion that this is exactly what has happened on several occasions in Quaker history and is happening again to British, but not world, Quakerism. It seems strange that some Friends can dispense with Christianity so effortlessly, in direct abandonment of 300 years of the history, tradition and witness of their Society, the beliefs and writings of its founders and its very *raison d'être*. This is perhaps a microcosm of the English rejection of institutional religion, the Christianity of the 'founders' of modern British society. Quakerism is becoming just another '-ism' for a disparate group of friendly, peaceable people who like a bit of quiet on a Sunday morning. Currently it is offering Christ without a cross; humankind without sin; and a shared silence with no uniting theology to underpin it. Quaker opposition to creeds – creeds are too often rigid, unbending, arcane and create insiders and outsiders – can be justified from church history. Unfortunately the Religious Society of Friends has confused this with *de facto* opposition to theology, which might have clarified its discourse and inspired its outreach.

In this situation, there is no doctrine left to indoctrinate – in the value-neutral sense of the term. Whether this will work to the advantage of Quakers in membership and survival terms remains to be seen. The erosion of Christianity within the Society is in part a failure of education, which is also germane to our inquiry. There is no discipline of confirmation classes for intending members and the religious or spiritual education of Friends is dependent on their opting in to residential courses and discussion groups or choosing books from the meeting-house library – or not. Even a successful leisure activity requires disciplined application. The consequences of excising a clergy along with their teaching ministry are the enhancement of individualism and the reduction of a sense of the corpus, the body of believers. In British society, in which everyone prizes being able to believe whatever they like, is there any point in joining a special friendly society to do it?

What this process also illustrates extremely well for our purposes, however, is the way in which a secular mindset can enter a religious organization, displace the originating religious – in this case Christian – language and rapidly become the norm. The narrowing of language leads in the longer term to the narrowing of mind. In the long term, this is the potential loss not just of Christianity but of God. It is a re-run of Moncure Conway (see p. 24). There will be some inside an organization like this genuinely unable to see what has happened or even to appreciate that there is a problem. That is the extent of the 'infection' when a beguiling secular humanism encounters a friendly, uncritical and genuine group of seekers after truth. George Fox, in contrast, was a seeker who became a *finder*. Or rather, as he would have said, he was found.

It is easy to castigate a group like the Religious Society of Friends where the process of secularization and loss of theism can be so easily traced, as it has reached the centre of the Society's life and visibly infected its official publications. It resembles a highly effective computer virus wiping the hard drive of its content. But one might ponder to what extent this same process is happening among individuals, including the clergy, in other churches. How far does this connect with the fact that the liberal churches are experiencing more rapid decline than their conservative counterparts? Is there no alternative somewhere between liberal humanism with a bit of heritage Christianity thrown in and conservative fundamentalist reaction? How far are the churches taking the education of their own members seriously? How far are their members willing to let them, in terms of committing their time and effort?

W. E. Sangster, writing about Methodist decline even before the Second World War, believed that one reason for this decline lay in Methodism letting go of its weekly class meetings in members' homes.[23] He likened these to the cells of a honeycomb. They were a mixture of Bible study, prayer, self-examination, pastoral support and social encounter, with a group of about twelve under lay leadership. Sangster pinpointed other causes for the decline of the churches. One was the effect of the Great War – people asking why God had not stopped it. He found a loss of confidence in preaching the Bible amoung preachers who were telling people what not to believe, or thinking their own doubts aloud in the pulpit, rather than telling congregations what to believe. He noted many of the social changes we have seen before: 'counter attractions' on Sunday, the 'wireless', migration to new areas, which broke church ties, and the 'spirit of secularism'.[24]

It is hard to know to what extent the churches are currently addressing what is happening in this national picture, which Sangster alone demonstrates they have known about for 60 years, or to what extent they are busily rearranging deckchairs on the *Titanic*. Moreover, it is hard to see what they can do about it, even if they are keenly aware of what is going on. Cultures can suddenly change, but not often, as will be discussed in Chapter 6. Faced with the grim attendance statistics, the churches can respond in a number of ways, as categorized by Toynbee: archaism, the retreat into the past; futurism, building castles in the air; mysticism, the retreat into inner mysteries; or re-formation, using the crisis to plan new beginnings.[25]

Writing an outline for a book from his prison cell, Dietrich Bonhoeffer talked of religionless humankind that has 'come of age'. *Homo religiosus* is in terminal decline, and Christianity needs to understand and present itself as not a religion, but, as Barth argued, as the antithesis of religion. Humankind, claimed Bonhoeffer, can protect itself against all forces except one – itself. 'God' as an idea, a working hypothesis, as a stop-gap for our embarrassments, has become superfluous. This 'God' is an abstract argument, and has been forced out of the world as unnecessary, redundant. We have to learn to live without this 'God', who is a sort of prop for the weak. 'Religious people speak of God when human knowledge (or perhaps because they are simply too lazy to think) has come to an end . . . In fact it is always the *deus ex machina* they bring on the scene.'[26] Far from being a disaster for Christianity, the loss of this 'God' clears the decks for an understanding of the living God, the God encountered in Jesus Christ. He is 'the centre of life'. 'We are to find God in what we know, not in what we don't know . . .'[27] But if Bonhoeffer embraced secularization, he did not condone privatized religion:

> The displacement of God from the world, and from the public part of human life, led to the attempt to keep his place secure at least in the sphere of the 'personal', the 'inner', and the 'private' . . . The secrets of [a person's] intimate life, from prayer to sexual life – have become the hunting ground of modern pastoral workers. In that way they resemble . . . the dirtiest gutter journalists . . .[28]

Privatized religion fails for Bonhoeffer for two reasons: in order to help people spiritually in a context of privatized religion, it is thought necessary to probe into their secret sins. Also it is thought that a person's essential nature is their inner life, when their essential nature should be their whole life.

The Death of Christian Britain is a provocative title for a book. Its author, Callum Brown, describes himself on his personal web site as an 'atheist-specialist in the social history of religion'. He is an evangelist for post-modern atheism and sees Europe as leading the world into post-modernity through liberation and two surviving but fluid central moral doctrines, respect for the body and respect for the planet. He delineates the rapid collapse of Christian culture from the 1960s and finds that the most important key to understanding the changing role of religion in a society is that of gender. This is more important than class or race in his view. The 'recrafting' of femininity from the 1960s meant that the pious, conformist religious identity assigned to mothers and daughters disappeared. Women had been the main constituency of church congregations, hence the sudden impact on institutional Christianity. Men's churchgoing, in contrast, was often in order to partner a woman, so with fewer women attending, male attendance also declined. Brown paints a bleak picture with which to draw to a close this assessment of Christian collapse. But is he right?

The surprising persistence of Christianity in the face of institutional decline

Adrian Hastings reminds us that 'the Church of Jane Austen was a profoundly secularized one', but yet out of it developed the vitality

of the nineteenth-century churches.[29] That was no small achieve-
ment, for the Enlightenment had brought scepticism about established institutions, raised the status of the natural sciences above that
of the human sciences and questioned the very basis of knowledge
itself. John Hull suggests that the Christian faith is still very much
on the European chessboard. It does not control the play but at least
it is not relegated to the box of captured pieces.[30] Wolffe assigns
Christianity a possible, though not inevitable, continuing role of
'prominence but not dominance' in twenty-first-century Britain.[31]
Abercrombie and Warde note that although formal religion is in
decline, the clergy are still listened to and 'their pronouncements can
generate considerable controversy'.[32] The way archbishops periodically pop up on TV and the continuing media interest in impending
papal and archiepiscopal appointments illustrate their point.

The 2001 national census included a question on religion that has
already been referred to. It is worth quoting the results, as summa-
rized by the Office for National Statistics. The numbers are in thousands.

Christian	42,079 or 71.6%
Buddhist	152 or 0.3%
Hindu	559 or 1.0%
Jewish	267 or 0.5%
Muslim	1,591 or 2.7%
Sikh	336 or 0.6%
Other religions	179 or 0.3 per cent
Total of all religions	**45,163 or 76.8%**
No religion	9,104 or 15.5%
Not stated	4,289 or 7.3%
Total of no religion/not stated	**13,626 or 23.2%**
Total population	**58,789 (100%)**

What do these figures mean? The census is legally compulsory, but
these are the categories in which people chose to record themselves.
So according to the self-descriptions of its people, Britain is not secular. Indeed, on the best interpretation of these figures from the point
of view of believers, only 15.5 per cent of the nation have definitely
shed religion altogether. Some of the 'not stated' people could also
be pro-religious, but might object to declaring their position on a

census return, perhaps even for biblical reasons (2 Samuel 24). One could even argue that in some sense the country is mainly Christian, certainly not 'post-Christian', although this might find scant favour with liberal intellectuals. But, of course, it could be urged that much of the Christianity hidden in these figures is nominal. Commentators unsympathetic to Christianity are apt to contrast these figures with the disputed figure of 7 or 8 per cent of regular church attenders. But these figures are by no means isolated. A telephone poll of 1,045 adults undertaken by Populus for *The Times* newspaper in April 2004 found that 63 per cent thought of Britain as being a Christian country and 55 per cent 'personally believe that the Easter story that Jesus rose from the dead is true', while 37 per cent claimed they would attend a church service at some point over Easter.[33] What the figures cannot reveal is the number of people whose mindset or religious values have become secularized, whatever their stated religious affiliation. Are we looking at a country and culture in which Christianity has lost its nerve?

Looking at wider aspects of culture than statistics, David Lyon argues that secularization is contingent on modernity and modernity is now itself in question.[34] In this situation 'Reason loses its capital R, science softens its hard edges, and knowledge is seen – and felt – as (con)textual, local and relative'.[35] For Lyon the ascendancy of science over religion is itself a meta-narrative that has now fallen on hard times. He uses the metaphor of Jesus in Disneyland (drawn from a real Christian event staged in Disneyland, California), in which the real and the unreal, the modern and the post-modern are all blurred. Disneyland is a social and cultural symbol of our times. Its influence is global and its characters are recognizable across cultures. The experience it provides is about illusion, fantasy, revised realities, multiple meanings, with play and pleasure as its centre. He calls the preference for the Disney version over the 'real' thing, e.g. for Mickey Mouse over a 'real' mouse, 'Disneyfication'. Disney has, remarkably, even swallowed up and Americanized the quintessentially English Winnie the Pooh, who went on to be hailed in Melbourne, Australia as a 'United Nations ambassador for friendship'.[36] Poor Pooh.

Lyon turns to the UK and examines those Christians 'who choose to believe but not identify with believers'.[37] They construct their personal pack of beliefs, choosing some, rejecting others. This is part of a process not so much of secularization as 'the sacralization of the self'. Matthew Arnold's 'Dover Beach', so often cited in loss-of-faith accounts, is to Lyon no more than 'blithely blinkered Eurocentrism'. Europeans, who have problems handling religion, are projecting these on to the world stage. The secularization of scholarship preceded the scholarship of secularization. That is to say, religion has become lost from view in accounts of the modern world. 'Some secularization scholarship may well be tainted with anti-religious assumptions.'[38]

What about that 71.6 per cent of the UK population who claim to be Christian? Brierley estimates that 8 million people in England still enter a church at least once per year. Wedding and funeral attendances are included in this computation. The total number of attendances in a year is estimated at 213 million compared to 25 million for football, but when statistics reach this point they start to look like the number of passenger rail journeys or miles per annum: hard to think of in terms of people.

Growth has continued in Christian groups that are perceived as 'unreasonable', i.e. fundamentalist and biblically conservative. There are also local exceptions to the trend of decline. Do these exceptions exhibit a common 'success formula'? At an individual level, some churches are thriving. The Kingsway International Christian Centre (KICC) in Hackney (Pentecostal), led by the Revd Matthew Ashimolowo, started in 1992 with a congregation of 200 which by 1999 had grown to more than 6,000. Holy Trinity, Brompton (Church of England), saw its Alpha Courses grow to reach more than 20,000 annually worldwide, within seven years of establishing them. 'New Churches', which include what used to be called house churches, grew by 161 per cent between 1979 and 1989 and again by 38 per cent between 1989 and 1998, with Sunday attendances estimated at 230,500. These are net figures, as New Churches experience the curious phenomenon of many people leaving as well. Moreover, they are not really a composite but an umbrella grouping which embraces various strands, estimated by Brierley as numbering at least twenty.[39] Independent Baptist churches have continued to grow strongly and the Baptist Union of Great Britain, which represents 81 per cent of Baptist churches, experienced a modest growth of 2 per cent in the decade to 1998.

At the liberal end of the Christian spectrum, Brierley estimates

Quaker attendance (as opposed to membership) to have increased in the decade to 1998 by 110 per cent (numerically the average Sunday attendance is 8,600). Of this number, 47 per cent is by transfer growth, largely from the Church of England, and 38 per cent by unchurched people accessing Quaker spirituality. He points out that the latter category is transient. Many do not stay for long. As we have already noted (pp. 57ff.), the question here is whether people are accessing Quakerism because it is a different Christian grouping or because it has ceased to be Christian.

It is the Baptists, Pentecostals and New Churches who have the highest percentages of 'twicers' (those who attend twice on Sunday): 22, 33 and 36 per cent respectively. Zygmunt Bauman is not surprised by the vitality of fundamentalism. He sees it as a legitimate child of post-modernity, promoting the feeling of many people that they are being told authoritatively by the culture not to believe and offered instead a perplexing freedom. '[Fundamentalism] emancipates the converted from the agonies of choice.'[40] But it does it at a price, by abolishing freedom and providing an 'alternative rationality'.

There is also a regional element in how far Christianity is, or is not, prospering. The south-east is faring better than the north and the west. In the south-east 40 per cent of the nation's churchgoing occurs, but only 37 per cent of the total population resides. The biggest drop in churchgoing has occured in two very different areas socially, the West Midlands and East Anglia, but East Anglia has the highest regional percentage of 'twicers', 20 per cent of all church attendances there.

Conservative Christians in the USA have mobilized the media, creating their own TV and radio stations to spread the message. The only licensed interdenominational radio station broadcasting in the UK, as opposed to those arriving by satellite, is Premier Radio. This is part of the Premier Media Group, which also includes Premier Online and Lifeline, a telephone helpline. It aims to provide 'a distinctively Christian radio station which is commercially successful and true to its commitment'. The target audience is churchgoers, lapsed churchgoers and people 'sympathetic to Christian values' including belief in God but with no church background. The programmes comprise news and lifestyle items, Christian commentary, phone-ins and a range of Christian music, leaning towards the evangelical end of the spectrum.

There is also evidence of the persistence of institutional Christianity in far less predictable or headline-grabbing ways. What follows is just one example. In the nineteenth century, Wesleyan Methodism was the parent denomination among various Methodist denominations. Its governing body of clergy, the annual Conference, was under the very firm hand of the Reverend Jabez Bunting (1779–1858). He was a 'high' Methodist, an organizer and manager, who accumulated power in many Methodist departments: mission, publications, Conference, and theological education for ministers. Unlike other ministers, who had to submit to being moved around by Conference as part of a compulsory itinerancy, he was allowed to remain in London from 1833 at Wesleyan Methodist headquarters. Bunting undoubtedly consolidated the young Wesleyan Methodist society into a church. But his power, his manner and his favoured status made enemies. A series of anonymous pamphlets began to circulate against him from the mid-1830s. They continued, steadily increasing in venom until even more vituperative 'Fly Sheets' were mailed to every minister in 1845.

Minister and former bookseller James Everett was suspected of being the author, but he never admitted this. The pamphlets were written in his style. He certainly paid for the printing. Everyone knew that much. The circumstantial evidence against him was very strong. Conference of 1847 asked all ministers, Everett included, to sign a statement that they had nothing to do with the scurrilous Fly Sheets. Two hundred and fifty-six ministers, including Everett, refused. After this impasse, the Fly Sheets and, in addition, abusive contra-pamphlets continued. By 1849 Conference had had enough. It was determined to expel the people responsible for the Fly Sheets. Everett was summoned in full Conference and publicly asked whether he were the author. He refused to answer. He was expelled, along with two other ministers, William Griffith, who had probably read the Fly Sheet proofs, and Samuel Dunn, who had nothing to do with them. Dunn and Griffith were known modernizers, who wanted a more representative Conference, including elected lay people, with a limit to the power of the 'platform' party that included Bunting.

Expelling all three was a tactical mistake. The expelled ministers lobbied their cause among the Wesleyan Methodist people, many of whom were already enthusiastic for church reform in a more democratic direction. As a result, in the five years up to 1855, 100,469 members left Wesleyan Methodism, a third of its total membership. This figure excluded 'attenders' who left, those not in formal membership of the church but who worshipped regularly in local congregations. Some joined the Primitive Methodists, some the Congregationalists, others what became in 1857 the United Free Methodist Church. Some no doubt ceased to attend any place of worship, not an uncommon response after religious friction. These withdrawals, by allowing Bunting even more authority among the remaining Wesleyan Methodists, permitted him to position Wesleyan Methodism as a *via media* between nonconformity and the Church of England. In that sense he won, but at a very high price. The whole affair is in many ways a piece of unchristian church history.

What has this nineteenth-century dispute and schism within Wesleyan Methodism to do with the twenty-first century? Simply that as another result of the fall-out of those 100,469 members, a new denomination was born, the Wesleyan Reform Union (WRU). It still survives. Its website details its member churches. It was never a comprehensive national church and its geographical concentration is mainly in the south and west of the Yorkshire counties, Derbyshire and the Wellingborough area of Northamptonshire, with other chapels scattered throughout the country. According to 'reason' one would have expected it to wither away long ago or to have rejoined the parent body, the Methodist Church of Great Britain, perhaps at the time of the 1932 merger that brought together most of the British Methodist denominations. The other predictable option would have been to preserve its existence as a tribal remnant, brooding over that increasingly distant quarrel. In fact none of these things happened. The Wesleyan Reform Union has already outlived its much larger Wesleyan Methodist parent as a separate denomination by some 70 years, even though most people, including many mainstream Methodists, have never heard of it. Why?

Its web site affirms its origins in the Methodist family of churches, with the reason for its existence as church reform. The Confession of Faith adopted by its 1970 Conference positions the Union firmly within orthodox and evangelical but not charismatic Christian doctrine. The strong element of lay leadership, including lay presidency at communion services, seems to have stood it in good stead to survive with small congregations and few full-time ministers. There is a tradition of independence in the local churches. In 2003 there were 1,947 recorded members, a decrease of 56 on the previous year. Also in 2003, 22 of its churches recorded an increase in membership, 39 no change, while 48 churches saw a fall. Seventeen ministers are listed, seven of whom are retired. There were 131 lay preachers and 702 'scholars' (children in church education groups). Two additional ministers were recorded in training and one on probation. Individual church membership figures range from two at Froggatt, Derbyshire, to 75 at the Pastures Church in High Wycombe. Many churches have single-figure membership. (Once again, these figures do not include attenders not in formal membership.) Distance learning in biblical and theological studies is provided in association with two other small denominations, the Independent Methodists and the Countess of Huntingdon's Connexion (figures taken from the Wesleyan Reform Union 2003–04 Year Book).

By any reckoning this denomination should have died out a long time ago. But it did not. Membership is currently in decline at a rate of 3.3 per cent per annum, so unless that is arrested it must in time fade away. But that could have been said in 1855. For our purposes the WRU is not a model of Christian expansion or extrovert vitality – but it is one of unexpected persistence in the face of all the odds. There is a good possibility that this denomination will continue to survive, even though closure of some of its smaller chapels is highly likely in the coming decades. Significantly, the factors working against the WRU's survival have been social rather than theological. As the villages in which many of its chapels are found have ceased to be working villages, becoming dormitories and collections of holiday homes, the life blood of its congregations has ebbed away. In this situation the quality of the leadership at congregational level has proved to be a crucial factor in church survival. This denomination does not see its future in the past, in a re-entry to mainstream Methodism, which Wesleyan Reformers reckon is now too broad and too liberal, but in association with like-minded evangelical Christians and a continuing separate organizational identity. Even in Cawston, Norfolk, one of its most struggling circuits of churches (22 members spread across four churches), there is talk of church planting.

A more publicized feature of Christian persistence, and a recurring feature of church history, is revivalism. One of the most interesting revival movements of the late twentieth century began in 1994 at an airport. Lyon thinks the place itself was significant.[41] Airports are brightly lit, enclosed systems of steel and concrete buildings. Walking around them or along the long corridors to the waiting bays and boarding gates is an experience out of space and time. They have no outside reference points. Flights that arrive or depart at all hours create similar disorientation, as the building is artificially lit at all times. After an uncomfortable time on an aircraft, itself a strange tube-like contraption which inhibits free movement and whose windows are tiny relative to the structure, so that attention is directed to the interior, one emerges into a place which seems strangely similar – another airport. 'Was the flight real? Is this placeless space real?' But Pearson International Airport, Toronto, became the scene of the 'Toronto Blessing', which grew into an indigenous, widely networked local church, based on pentecostal phenomena promoted by means of the internet. By mid-1996 300,000 people had visited to learn more. In the UK, 4,000 churches were said to have been touched by the Blessing.[42] It was a high-tech version of outdoor preaching such as that of the Primitive Methodist revival.

Crucial to the assertion that Christianity in Britain is on the way out is the allegation that it is dying out among the young. Clearly, in terms of church contact, the young are largely unchurched. From 1996 onwards, several parallel research projects undertaken by the Religious Education Research Team at the University of Exeter School of Education and Lifelong Learning and collectively known as the Biblos project examined the knowledge, understanding and attitudes of young people towards the Bible and the person of Jesus. The methods used were pilot questionnaire, revised full questionnaire and semi-structured interviews with a selection of volunteers whose questionnaire answers reflected a range of the whole sample. Schools were chosen from all over the country: urban and rural, multi-ethnic and mono-ethnic, faith schools, community schools and independent schools. In the study of attitudes to Jesus, 542 Year 8 (age 12+) pupils took part. This age group is the year in which Jesus is most commonly taught at any length in RE lessons. In the examination of attitudes to the Bible, 722 pupils in Year 10 (age 14+) took part in the 2001 study; in the 2003 survey 1,066 pupils drawn from Year 6, the final year of primary schooling, Year 9 (age 13+) and Year 12, the lower sixth (age 16+) took part. The sample of students surveyed in 2003 reflected almost exactly the categories of religious adherence revealed in the 2001 national census (see p. 66), so the sample group can be viewed as very significant. This is therefore one of the most comprehensive clusters of surveys ever undertaken in this field. Analysis and further research are continuing, including studies in New Zealand to see whether there are particularly British factors which might have influenced the young people in the UK sample. Full research reports[43] and a stream of articles have been published from this work. We shall restrict ourselves to the particular findings that relate to secularization. Are British young people hostile to the Bible, or biblically illiterate, or both, as some commentators outside education assume?

The anonymous participants were asked about themselves: which religion if any they identified with; how often they attended worship, on a scale from 'never' to 'very often'; their interests and hobbies, including the types of books or magazines they read and the sorts of TV programmes they watched. In total 83.5 per cent of them identified with a specific religion (70.5 per cent Christianity). Only 19 per cent of males and 12 per cent of females said that they never attended a place of worship (the question embraced weddings and funerals). They were given three boxes in which to insert preferences for what 'mattered most' to them. Some stated more than three, some fewer, but all are included in this summary (the percentage of the whole 1,066 that cited each response is given):

Family	93.8%
Friends	88.0%
Activities/hobbies	51.3%
Education	36.5%
Other	20.5%
Religion	4.0%

Clearly the decline of British family life has not destroyed the family ideal. Year 9 pupils were the least likely to cite education as something that 'matters most'. How does the small 4 per cent of those to whom religion 'matters most' relate to the large 83.5 per cent identifying with a religion above? It could mean that the identification is genuine, but is not held to matter much. This resembles being in a motoring rescue organization – good in case the car breaks down and you are conscious of being in the AA or the RAC or Green Flag, but hardly a life-changing affiliation. Religion is perhaps seen as part of personal identity, without being a priority. But the numbers citing religion as something that 'matters most' rose from Year 6 to Year 9 and again to Year 12. One difficulty in interpreting this figure of 4 per cent is technical. It arises from the three-space answer box on the questionnaire: it does not indicate how many pupils might have put religion fourth or fifth or sixth in their list of what 'matters most'. Arguably, after family and friends, the adolescent has only one box left to fill! We have no means of knowing whether a very large percentage might have recorded religion as a fourth or fifth choice.

Despite the low number citing religion as a thing that 'matters most' there was no evidence of biblical illiteracy or of uniformly negative attitudes towards the Bible. Pupils thought that their family had shaped their attitudes to the Bible (27.4 per cent) or that their attitudes came from their own beliefs (14.5 per cent) or a life experience (8.8 per cent), from RE lessons (5.9 per cent) or a place of worship (3.9 per cent); 32.3 per cent thought that their family viewed the Bible as important or respected it. Another 7.9 per cent went further and stated their family believed it to be true. But about a third thought that their friends would take a negative view of it. By applying technical-analysis procedures and processes,[44] certain cultural profiles emerged from the data. Pupils who cited reading, voluntary work, youth groups or performing arts as their preferred hobbies were more likely to have a positive attitude towards the Bible than those who did not. Pupils who cited film, TV or cinema as a major hobby or interest were more likely to have a negative attitude to the Bible than those who did not. The same was true for those who listed personal computer games or magazines and car/motorbike magazines. In terms of TV, those who listed soaps or dramas as their favourite TV genre were more likely to have a positive attitude towards the Bible, whereas those who cited sport were more likely to have a negative attitude. Only 1.1 per cent did not own or did not watch TV. In terms of the more positive attitude scores, females outnumbered males. For instance, 73 per cent of females stated that they watched soaps or dramas compared to 33 per cent of males. As a soundbite one could say that young people who were into 'acts and facts' tended to be more negative towards the Bible while those were into 'human needs and long reads' were more positive.

Years 9 and 12 pupils in the survey were asked to consider pairs of semantically differentiated statements (e.g. 'The Bible is important to me') and 'The Bible is not important to me' and to tick 'agree strongly', 'agree' or 'not sure'. The list below combines the 'strongly agree' and 'agree' ticks into one total. This reveals something even more surprising for the secularization hypothesis:

The Bible is important to me	33.7 per cent
The Bible is relevant today	53.7 per cent
The Bible is interesting	35.9 per cent
The Bible contains truth	47.9 per cent
The Bible can show people how to live	63.1 per cent
I look to the Bible for personal guidance	18.7 per cent
I believe in the Bible	39.6 per cent
The Bible should be respected	74.1 per cent
The Bible has important things to say to people today	47.8 per cent

The results from this cluster of surveys do not deny empty churches. But they do furnish further evidence of religious adherence and perhaps surprisingly positive attitudes towards the Bible on the part of young unchurched people (as well as young members of religions other than Christianity) at key points in their schooling. Whether the imperative not to appear uncool in public would allow them to voice some of these sentiments in class, rather than privately in a questionnaire or alone with an interviewer, is perhaps open to question. Norman is nevertheless quite wrong to assert, with no supporting evidence, that 'the schools founded to teach Christianity to children are now often failing to do so'.[45] If we replace assertion with evidence, the case goes the other way, especially since another of the findings is that the church-school children tend to be more positive towards Christianity and the Bible.

These surveys represent work with young people at school. What lies beyond? A significant qualitative research study, 'Christianity on Campus', was undertaken in 2003 in a southern UK university by Claire Copley. Her hypothesis was that with widening access to higher education, a profile of the student body might reflect the attitudes of young adults in wider society. By questioning a number of them who might be presumed to be articulate a window might be gained on to the whole. After a pilot study, she used three slightly differing but detailed questionnaires for members of the student body who were members of the Christian Union, members of the joint Methodist-Anglican society and a student sample who were members of no student religious group. All represented a wide range of degree subjects. Semi-structured interviews followed with a cross-section of respondents and, in the case of student religious societies, longitudinal observation of their meetings over the period of a year. The questions covered personal background and history of links with religion, if any; beliefs and values about ultimate reality, human nature, Jesus, the Bible, and life after death; particular moral issues; and what a person should do or believe in order to be reck-oned a Christian.

The most interesting of the three samples from the point of view of our inquiry is those students unaffiliated to any university Christian group. How secular are they? In this sample, 3 per cent belonged to a religion other than Christianity, well below the 2001 census figure for this group; 47 per cent of them identified with Christianity. Only 20 per cent of this same sample identified with atheism and 23 per cent with agnosticism. In other words the atheist and agnostic total was only 43 per cent of the non-affiliated students, still a minority. Unsurprisingly, this unaffiliated sample rated friends and family more highly as sources of guidance than any Christian sources such as church, chaplaincy or Bible. While 20 per cent believed in a personal God and a further 20 per cent held that some sort of spiritual or vital force controls life, 26 per cent rejected any god or spiritual guiding force. They viewed human nature positively rather than as fallen or lost. Jesus was a wise moral teacher (36 per cent), sent by God for a specific purpose (13 per cent). Humans are autonomous and free to make their own future, with or without God (80 per cent). Evil consists of harmful human attitudes (46 per cent). After death there is bodily resurrection (6 per cent), the soul or spirit passes on (36 per cent), there is nothing (23 per cent) or we don't know (23 per cent, other categories bringing the total to 100). Attitudes towards homosexuality were more negative than those expressed by affiliated Christian students. Adultery was always wrong (40 per cent). Premarital sex was 'not wrong at all' (66 per cent). There was 'nothing wrong at all' with excessive drinking (23 per cent). More were opposed to abortion than in the liberal

Christian group sample (Methodist-Anglican). What identifies a Christian (respondents were permitted to select more than one category) is citizenship of a Christian country (6 per cent), being baptized (23 per cent), being 'born again' (10 per cent), confessing Jesus Christ as Saviour (56 per cent), following Jesus' teachings (53 per cent, a higher percentage response than that of students affiliated to university Christian groups). This is part of one qualitative survey, conducted in one university, whose full results have yet to appear. It is important therefore to extrapolate with care from the findings. What it shows, however, is that even among the young, attitudes towards religion are not overwhelmingly negative. One might conclude that despite the bombast of secular thinking, religious beliefs show themselves to be surprisingly tenacious.

The Church of England, even though it is in decline, is another feature in the persistence of Christianity. The Church of England is quintessentially English. Thomas Gray's 'Elegy Written in a Country Churchyard' (1751) encapsulates much of this idea. The 'C of E' is unimaginable in any other context than England, except in far-off places where English emigrés pine for home. The sound of church bells for evensong on a summer Sunday evening, the Festival of Nine Lessons and Carols, the gloriously Trollopian titles of Right Reverend, Very Reverend, Most Reverend and Venerable, the miscellany of deans, archdeacons, precentors, prebendaries and all the rest are endearingly English. Senior Anglican bishops are still social barons in English society. Moreover, the Church of England still attempts to be a national church, with a presence in every settlement of size. It is active as a supporter, promoter and patron of the arts and culture, including English arts and culture. Although it has been tormented and weakened by controversies over the ordination of women, gay priests and bishops and reforming its service book, it remains an unusual mixture of reason, the gentle promotion of Christian belief and a spirituality stretching into the pre-Reformation past of the church in England. At the extremes of Anglo-Catholicism and evangelical Anglicanism, the Church of England is, like some of its clergy, decidedly eccentric. But 'there will probably never be an Anglican suicide bomber' (a comment attributed to journalist Rod Liddle).

Yet the Church of England is more than a curio of English culture and more than a national denomination with the biggest membership 'on paper'. It is a major stakeholder in education, whose schools seem more popular than ever. Twenty-five per cent of all state-supported primary schools are Anglican. These contain 18 per cent of the nation's primary age school-children. Six per cent of state-supported secondary schools are Anglican and these contain 5 per cent of all secondary-school pupils. In addition, an estimated 1,000 out of 1,300 independent schools have a Church of England foundation or ethos. So a significant percentage of the nation's children pass through church schools for part of their education. They do not replace the 'lost' Sunday-school children but they are still a very large group. This is an opportunity for mission, for nurture or for the more delicate task of presenting the case for a religious way of life, specifically a Christian way of life, without coercion.

This possibility looks stronger in theory than it might be in practice. The staff rooms of voluntary controlled schools may contain people merely 'sympathetic' to church schools; only in voluntary aided (VA) schools is it legally permitted to question teachers at interview about their religious beliefs and practice. Church-school staff rooms are not necessarily the bastions of Christianity that some people in the pews might suppose or hope for. The same range of secularized thinking, adherence and sheer perplexity or ignorance on matters religious that can be found anywhere will be found in a school staff room. The vicar's weekly visit, often to lead collective worship, may be beneficial and welcome – or not. But at the very least the church school provides an opportunity to remove prejudice and misunderstanding about religions and impart accurate perspectives on what it means to take faith, especially Christian faith, seriously. Attitudes at Anglican church schools have shifted, from a tendency to emphasize their commonality with county schools (now called community schools) in the 1960s and 1970s, to a tendency to emphasize their distinctiveness or separateness. Why are they so popular? Is it simply because their test and league-table results tend to be better and middle-class parents are playing the field? Or have they become the modern heirs of the Sunday school to which parents would 'send' their children 60 years ago? That is to say, are they promoting broadly Christian values that are recognized by their client-parents to be worthwhile? In a cynical culture, the former reason – playing the system – will appeal as an explanation. But such cynicism may reflect more of the culture than the truth.

The Roman Catholic Church also has its own schools and at one time had the unofficial target slogan 'Every Catholic child to be taught by a Catholic teacher in a Catholic school'. There are 1,817 RC primary schools, 378 secondaries and 16 sixth-form colleges. Like the Church of England, the Roman Catholic Church is also the founding body or sponsor for various independent schools, 163 in all. When all the students in both sectors and all types of RC school are added together, they total 825,306.[46] In addition to this, other denominations have schools, e.g. Methodists, Quakers, Seventh Day Adventists. So do other religions, including Judaism, Islam and Sikhism. So the Christian and wider religious presence in education is significant.

Secularists, some other atheists and some Christians are opposed to faith schools as divisive. The Church of England, in its attempt to be a national church, can plead 'not guilty' to this charge. Its schools are open to children of other faiths and in some areas contain a majority of, say, Muslim pupils, whose religion is respected and in some cases practised in the school. Sometimes the church primary school doubles as the neighbourhood school. This can be the case in rural areas. Where schools are over-subscribed and priority is therefore given by governors to the children of churchgoing parents, church schooling becomes more controversial, although in a free-market economy, the simple and logical solution is to provide more church schools. Secularists favour community schools for all as being more integrative and often refer to them as 'neutral', as opposed to 'sectarian'. But few church schools operate in a manner that sociologists would recognize as sectarian and no community schools are neutral. A 'neutral' school is a secular (i.e. non-religious, as opposed to secularist) foundation school. The church school's values are 'up front'. The 'neutral', i.e. secular, school needs to specify its values explicitly. Of course, legally, in the free market anyone could perfectly easily open an atheistic or secularist foundation school. It would be certain to attract parents. But how many?

Education provides further evidence for the persistence of religiouse literacy, if not so much of religious affiliation. Recent years have witnessed an explosion in external examination entries in religious studies (RS), in GCSE, AS and A2 levels. In the period 1997–2001, short-course GCSE entries rose from 12,367 to 167,443. Entries for the full GCSE moved steadily from 118,776 to 120,354.

But by 2003 the total for long- and short-course GCSE entries exceeded 350,000. This means that more students are taking RS at age 16 than history (218,565), geography (232,830) or French (331,089). These figures have started to impact on AS and A2 entries post-16, especially where the popular student option of religion, ethics and philosophy is offered. The GCSE figures are not all student options. In some schools the standard 'RE for all' course has been switched to the short-course GCSE, to give all students an external qualification. So not all these candidates have chosen RS in preference to other subjects and not all are happy to be doing it. It is part of their curriculum portfolio. But these figures clearly show a number of things. One is that where options exist, RS proves a popular choice when it offers certain syllabuses. Another is that we cannot talk about the religious illiteracy of the young on a total examination-entry figure exceeded only by English, maths, science, and design and technology. At individual school level, some schools are still a desert for RE and some headteachers are deliberately allowing the subject to wither. There are not nearly enough specialist RE teachers or examiners for the growing GCSE numbers. The shortage is not much less than a crisis and the wilful ignoring of this by successive governments is not much less than a scandal. But the study of religion is alive and well with older secondary students, even if religious commitment is not.

It is difficult to make sense of the rich but conflicting evidence about religion in Britain, particularly the Christian religion. Those who would welcome the demise of religion can find plenty of evidence. Those who wish to see its survival can find some solace. Projection into the future is a difficult and uncertain exercise, for at no point in recent British history could anyone really have predicted society 100 years ahead, or even 50. We cannot know what is round the corner. The decline of the churches is not universal, but it is no less real or widespread because of the exceptions. Some denominations may disappear altogether in the years ahead. But it is a characteristic of Christianity that others may be born. A religion that proclaims the real and total death of its founder proclaims also his resurrection. Churches too, as denominations or as local congregations, can die. But then in new forms and different places, they can be born again. The other religions constitute a smaller minority numerically, but no one talks of them as likely to die out. In fact, if anything, they are likely to increase in numbers, Islam especially. It is possible that Christian discourse is being preserved in the schools, not just in church schools, even though Christianity is no longer taught as 'true' in all schools, but rather as one religion among many. To investigate this we have to examine more closely what is going on in syllabuses and classrooms. But before that, it is important to turn to another dimension of the British scene and that is the dimension of spirituality. Spirituality is often looked upon with more favour than religion. Could it be that religion will die while spirituality will live?

4

Spiritual Fruits, not Religious Nuts:
Replacing 'Religion' with 'Spirituality'

God wants spiritual fruits not religious nuts.
(Car window sticker, 2004)

A society like ours that finds religion hard to handle seems somehow
to live much more easily with spirituality. Perhaps this is because, as
a result of their history and culture, Europeans have come to associ-
ate religions with authority structures that tell them what to believe
and how to behave. Spirituality, in contrast, is perceived to be a do-
it-yourself affair, as hard or as easy as you want to make it. Like
Lycra underwear according to its advertising claims, spirituality can
mould itself to fit any personal contours. It is assumed that individuals are expected to conform to a religion and its doctrines: religion
is perceived as a take-it-or-leave-it affair. You fit in or you don't.
Spirituality is the bespoke tailoring of the personal life, with oneself
as the tailor. Spirituality is moving all the time and cannot be captured in a net or formula.

One meaning of the word 'definition' is 'the action or power of
making definite or clear' (*Dictionary of the English Language*,
Longman, 1984). Spirituality seems by its nature to lie outside the
boundary of definition; it can be made neither definite nor 100 per
cent clear. Religions in contrast are too often defined and frequently
made to appear like static belief systems. Religions seem to threaten
us by telling us what the meaning of life is and what our place is in
the grand scheme of things. The role allocated to us is to co-operate
or not. That is our only choice. Spirituality enables us to define what
life is all about and what we want to be – we build our own universe,
just like God. We have infinite choices. This is beautifully post-modern, since post-modernity no longer recognizes grand schemes of
things. Western society has assigned to religions a definition which

makes them look distinctly unappealing; though it is questionable whether this definition corresponds to the complexity of religions as they really are across the planet.

Moreover, on the surface spirituality is more eclectic than religion, allowing for a personal pick and mix of beliefs and practice. This aspect too finds readier favour than religion in an individualistic culture. Thus I might read 1 Corinthians 13 regularly for its inspirational words, practise yoga once a week to train body and mind, visit a clairvoyant to discuss my future, place a protective St Christopher talisman in my car and fast for a day or two in Ramadan to remember the poor. Or I might not bother with anything in particular, except to assent within myself to the 'more than': that there is more to life than the material, more than the immediate, more than meets the eye, more than the body and its needs. That's spirituality: we can choose action or inaction and nobody has any authority to say that what we are doing or not doing is wrong. The concept of the 'more than' takes some of the guilt out of individualistic materialism.

What this all means is that when spirituality in the west appears in a religionless guise, it looks dangerously like becoming either the moral exaltation of the self or else a synonym for the aesthetic. I say 'self-exaltation' because the self is at the centre of western spiritual exercises when they are divorced from religion. The self expects to be titillated, enlarged, enhanced, affirmed, as a result of the exercise. Much that currently passes for spirituality is therefore unashamedly secular in content. Having rejected a God-centred approach, it has become self-centred instead. It is sometimes no more than the inner-being equivalent of a choice of perfume or aftershave for the outer being. Or it is the aesthetic experience of responding to fine art or music or a seascape at sunset.

The self-deception latent in some secular approaches to spirituality might appear to drive spirituality into the arms of religion. That is no easy conclusion, for western perceptions of religion make its 'arms' unwelcoming, even repugnant, to many people of integrity who cannot subscribe to religious beliefs. But can we really conceive of an out-and-out atheistic spirituality? Or if we did, might atheists see themselves being dragged up the church or religious path by such a widely embracing idea? The answer has to be that despite the danger that it transposes into an exaltation of the self, we can emphatically conceive of a non-theistic, if not entirely atheistic, spirituality for two reasons. The first is that it would be just as arrogant of religions to claim a monopoly of spirituality as for them to claim a monopoly of morality and moral values. The second is that Buddhism is a living case study of a non-theistic approach to spirituality or, at least, one in which the theistic component is neither central nor compulsory nor universal. An entirely atheistic spirituality is hard to conceive, simply because atheism involves at least as much dogma and certainty as religion. But it cannot be ruled out. Nye and Hay argue that spirituality can be placed on a spectrum of meaning that runs from 'moral sensitivity' on the one hand to mystical union with God on the other.[1] In that sense religion is an institutional manifestation of spirituality. Or could it equally mean that spirituality is really an experiential manifestation of religion? In the cultures of Europe, spirituality and religion seem to be perceived as friend and foe, the one enabling, the other limiting and prescribing. This is a very serious misconception, operating to the detriment of both. These assumptions about their antithetical positions are not a universal feature of human culture. Europe could have got it wrong. But the result of the current discourse and one minor proof of its invalidity is that most people would be complimented if they were described as spiritual but would be much more ambivalent about being described as religious.

As we have seen, the spiritual may by its nature elude definition, but that can also provide an excuse for a lot of vague thinking and imprecision in the discourse about it. We seem to define religions too clearly while the spiritual remains much more of a fudge. Religions are subject to a searching spotlight of analysis and critical comment because we have come to believe that they can be defined and must be not only open to reason, but subject to it. Doctrine seems to provide evidence for this view, because by the formulation of doctrine religions succumb to the temptation to define themselves. This definition creates the possibility of contra-definition, challenge, debate. No right-minded religious believer could object to that. In the end religions may be found to be as unyielding to the attempt at definition as the spiritual. But that is not how they are perceived. For example, many people are prepared to offer their thoughts as to what Christianity 'all boils down to'. But spirituality is exempt from the cultural rules that religion is obliged to adhere to in submitting to definition and stringent criticism. Spirituality has become so personal, so private, so precious that it is not expected to be critiqued by the same rules and on the same terms as are applied to religion. Criticizing someone's spirituality is tantamount to critiquing their sex life, a shocking invasion of the personal – but it is far more acceptable to challenge their religious views. Thus a situation has arisen whereby Europeans are simultaneously severe on religions and lax on the spiritual. Any slipshod thinking passes as acceptable in the sphere of the spiritual while the most careful exposition of alleged religious, especially Christian, truth is subject to withering scrutiny.

Religious has come to have overtones of religiose, pious, devout, other-worldly or in some cases fanatical. Religion has become socially embarrassing. We have already referred to the conversation-stopping ability of those whose career is religion, should they hazard to reveal this at a party (see p. xiii). This is not a recent phenomenon in British society. Catherine Booth, co-founder of the Salvation Army together with her husband, William, pointed out in 1896 that people's way of talking changes when it comes to religion. There is a stiffness connected to the subject and even a different tone of voice, look and manner. Her view was that the English have suppressed their feelings about religion, reducing it to a non-feeling, cerebral assent to doctrine. 'If you have not got the right kind of feeling, I am afraid that you have not the right kind of religion.'[2]

In the face of the difficulties surrounding the notion of religion, some people wonder if we should be ready to surrender the word 'religion' altogether and replace it with 'spirituality'. Religious education in schools would therefore be restyled something like 'spiritual and moral education'. In the 1970s, one Oxfordshire secondary school experimented with the name 'the Art of Living'. Who is qualified to teach or examine or inspect *that*? Moreover, should educators be easing and endorsing a national embarrassment about religion, or rather correcting a false and stereotypical view of it and helping people to recognize that the problem of religion is directly connected with how it is perceived in western culture? This is also the explanation of why religion is not a 'problem' across the entire planet, because other cultures do not view it or describe it in that way. In other words the problem is intrinsic to one cultural pattern, not intrinsic to religion.

For 'religion' and 'spirituality' are not synonyms. Abolishing religion in favour of spirituality would be much more than the replacement of one word with another. It would close down whole avenues of belief, practice and truth claims. If we abolish the terminology of religion, we eventually deprive people of the concepts and thus in turn the feelings and the beliefs and the option of commitment. Why should religious education, or education as a whole, enable people to evade religious truth claims and run away to hide in something resembling a priest hole of the mind? Education does not always have to be about making people cosy; it can exercise a prophetic function as well, in other words it can call people to reconsider their entrenched attitudes and values or see how their culture might have programmed them into certain modes of thought. Of course, 'religion' is at least in part a western construct. Hindus did not see themselves as Hindus until the label was pinned on them, from the west. They were concerned with *sanatan dharma*. Religions across the planet are constantly evolving, never static, always adapting to cultures and eras, spaces and places, even though they have constants such as Torah and Qur'an, Guru Nanak and the Buddha. The word 'religion' itself has no magic. But that does not mean that the word 'spirituality' could simply replace or subsume it to ease European embarrassment.

Religions should not simply be portrayed as cold and cerebral schemata of beliefs or doctrine. Many 'religious' people do not see religion as an optional category of belief, but as a complete way of life, so much so that to outsiders 'believers' can sometimes appear very casual about their actual beliefs. Nor can a case be made for the moral badness of religion. Despite allegations, it would be hard to identify a case of any war that was caused entirely by religion with no other contributory factor. Religion is morally neutral in its planetary effects. If it has been one factor in some wars, it has been one factor in some peacemaking. If 'religion' produced the Inquisition, it also produced Mother Teresa. If it produced some very worldly medieval popes, it also produced the Franciscan friars. Religion can go 'hand in hand with a perception of ever-deepening awareness of the symbolic and imaginative orders'.[3] It is linked, as Coleridge saw, with the creative imagination. Even religious doctrine finds its spirited defenders:

> The notion of dogma terrifies men who do not understand the Church. They cannot conceive that a religious doctrine may be

clothed in a clear, definite and authoritative statement without at once becoming static, rigid and inert and losing all its vitality. In their frantic anxiety to escape from any such conception they take refuge in a system of beliefs that is vague and fluid, a system in which truths pass like mists and waver and vary like shadows. They make their own personal selection of ghosts, in this pale, indefinite twilight of the mind.[4]

'Their own personal selection of ghosts' might be seen as the weakness of much spirituality. Where does spirituality end and religion begin? There is no dividing line.

When I visit my wife's grave, I notice a recent grave close by with a simple oak cross bearing the one word 'Mandy' inscribed on a brass plate. I do not know who Mandy was, or when she lived and died. She was less than 27 years old when she died, as one of the many pots and bunches of flowers regularly placed there had a note to her, signed by a friend, recording the 27th birthday Mandy never reached. She must have left a small child or children, for infant-type drawings 'for mummy' are from time to time hung from the arms of the cross. The friend or family member takes the trouble to laminate these offerings against the weather. Presumably they believe, or the children believe, or they want the children to believe, that Mandy can in some way receive these little gifts or know about them. So Mandy is gone, but not utterly dead. Is that belief spirituality or religion? Does it matter? Or has western culture attempted to sever the two forces of spirituality and religion to the detriment of both? If so, religion has been reduced to prescriptive beliefs and obedience, while spirituality is reduced to personal inclination with ephemeral and unclear beliefs. Would they be stronger and more credible if combined?

Whatever is at work behind those graveyard offerings is intensely personal. But to see spirituality as an entirely individual or personal phenomenon divorced from beliefs or group practice would be a serious mistake. Spirituality sometimes appears in popular or mass manifestations or in specific localities. Flowers now routinely mark fatal road-accident or murder sites, although this practice only developed in the UK in the late 1980s. Even a school bus stop was sanctified by tealight candles placed in memory of a pupil who used to catch the bus there and died suddenly.[5] The Hillsborough football deaths of 1989 and the Dunblane primary-school shootings of 1996 in which 16 people died provide examples of mass grief and mourning rituals with implicit beliefs attached. In order to sustain their argument, post-modernists and secularists have to rubbish such beliefs or present them as a lingering yet superficial peasant piety. Such a view is extremely patronizing. It does not accept the integrity of those holding these hard-to-define beliefs. The group or mass feelings on these occasions are real, if inarticulate, and the tears that are shed are real tears.

The death of Princess Diana occurred in Paris on 31 August 1997. The violent and unnecessary death of a young, beautiful and popular figure, arguably badly wronged by her husband as well, will always be a traumatic and truly tragic event. The interpretation of the ensuing mass mourning puzzled sociologists at the time and has done so since. Fifty million blooms were placed in her memory; 10,000 tons of flowers were laid outside Buckingham and Kensington Palaces in the first week after her death. Nothing remotely like that had been seen in London since 11 November 1920, when Whitehall was 12 feet deep in flowers from the public to mark the opening of Lutyens' Cenotaph for the dead of the Great War. The reaction to Diana's death constitutes a serious problem for those who are wedded to the secularization hypothesis. It cannot be claimed that the public response proves that the British are either Christian or religious, but it certainly suggests they are not secular or, in the main, atheists. Instead the aftermath was ambivalent, exactly like the British mentality on religion. The popular response and the customized funeral service indicate both beliefs, values and practice, although these are not always what are thought of as 'religious' in ways that institutional religions would own. Customized funeral services, not just for princesses but also for 'ordinary' people, are increasingly common. In these funerals, the bereaved play a part in planning and leading and choosing the songs, readings, etc., rather than just accepting the set service from the prayer book.

In the case of Diana's death, the role of the media was unusual. They were not prepared for what happened. They did not orchestrate the mass grief but instead had to follow it. They were also, allegedly, corporately complicit in her death by virtue of the role of the 'paparazzi' in pursuing her car into the Paris tunnel. In that sense Diana's death was a sort of 'death by publicity'.[6] Kensington Palace became 'a site associated with the holy dead'.[7] The shrine to Diana and Dodi at Harrods Knightsbridge store is still visited by many tourist-pilgrims. J. Walley notes in the Diana case the idea of a shrine at Althorp, of pilgrimage and religious devotion, arguing that these are 'a substitute' for religion.[8] This is old secular-speak. They *are* religion, but simply not the religion of the churches. P. Chandler takes it further, noting the use of wayside shrines, flowers, lights and offerings, but misses the adaptation of Emily Brontë's poem 'Last Lines' as one of the tributes.[9] One could add the thousands of prayer-type notes such as one might find on a cathedral prayer-request board:

Diana and Dodi

RIP

May you have as much fun in heaven

as you did in St Tropez

Many more of these messages presupposed that Diana was in some state of being to receive them. They find parallels in some of the verses inserted in local newspapers to commemorate the anniversaries of deaths. J. Davies sees the whole thing as a mass shared emotional experience that also embraced diverse racial ethnic and sexual identity.[10] Nationalist feelings were aroused too. Some of the Welsh felt excluded by the depiction of Diana as 'England's rose'. To thus equate themselves with the British was a recurrence of a long-standing trend in English culture. It escaped commentary at the time that, like a sleeping princess in a fairy tale, Diana was laid to rest on a lake island. The overtones of Avalon, Glastonbury and the Arthurian legend hint that, like storybook sleeping princesses, she will one day awaken.

At the time of her death, Diana was in 'a state of semi-detachment from the royal family'.[11] In her life, she was known to be interested in spiritual issues. Her views on these matters evolved. She was committed to what she called a 'religion of the heart', a form of humanitarianism which was far from atheistic and 'superbly adapted to late modernity'.[12] Not only did she meet Mother Teresa, but they admired each other. She claimed for herself a truer Christianity than that of a bishop whom she disliked.[13] She was an icon, itself a word with religious significance, for many things. Not least of these was a 'believing without belonging' view of religion, seen by Diana as a higher Christianity than that of the churches, a glorious mixture of experience, reason, exposure to different spiritual traditions, personal conviction and what one might bluntly call superstition. All in all, the death of Diana brought to the surface the complex mixture of spirituality and religious sentiment that is latent among the British.

Popular spirituality has other manifestations. It sometimes attributes inexplicable events to pseudo-human causes. R. A. Hinde discusses this tendency, taking 'Lady Luck' as an example.[14] He notes that Royal Air Force crews in the Second World War were prone to ascribe aircraft problems to 'gremlins', mischievous sprites which delighted in causing technical problems. Gremlins fulfilled a number of social functions. They dispelled by humour the tension or frustration caused perhaps by faulty workmanship on a repair. They deflected blame from individuals when things went wrong. They preserved relationships between flight and ground staff. They promoted group solidarity. But were they more? When a whole series of events inexplicably goes wrong, many people talk of being jinxed, meaning under a curse or bad spell. The word is probably derived from the *Jynx torquilla*, the wryneck, an innocent-looking and rare bird from the woodpecker family, at one time associated with witchcraft. Perhaps, like hot cross buns, the jinx is an example of secularization.

Popular spirituality has also been boosted by the shift in attitudes towards complementary medicine and practices such as yoga. This shift has removed them from the realm of the cranky and brought them into mainstream acceptability. The profusion of books on alternative and complementary therapies, and of shops devoted to selling allied products, reflects either a deep and non-rational interest in these matters or else the failure of western medicine with its rational potions and practice to deal with whole people. Aromatherapy, acupuncture, herbal medicine, reflexology and the rest often come with an associated 'life view' or set of guiding principles, however they might be scoffed at by some doctors. In contrast, the NHS prescription comes alone, in a hurry, with no life view and no magic except the mandatory illegible alchemic handwriting, which is fast becoming extinct with computer-generated scripts. No one who has been shunted through a five-minute interview in a doctor's surgery, which has taken weeks to arrange unless it is an emergency, can view the process as in any way affirmative of the whole person's well-being. That ignores the first barrier of getting through receptionists who put every obstacle in the way of granting appointments, presumably through abuse of the system by a minority of patients or extreme patient overload. The abandonment by many British GPs of emergency night visits to their patients and the contracting out of this service to agencies is another example of the depersonalization of health care. This is a desolating loss for those who are seriously or terminally ill in their own home, and for their carers. What price can be put on seeing the face of the doctor you know (who also knows you and your case history) when you are in agonizing pain in the middle of the night?

This is not to suggest that this is necessarily a failing or abdication of duty by doctors; rather it is part of a complex social and political process related to the economic consequences of an ageing population. Yet health remains a very personal matter, which does not lend itself to being depersonalized. Many people have anxieties about specific personal health problems or more vaguely about ill health in the future. Funerals, whether religious or secular, confront people with the reality and, humanly speaking at least, the absolute finality of death. We feel uneasy as we rise for the entry of the coffin to the place of worship or crematorium, because this awareness of death – crudely, the body in the box – challenges life in the way we live it every day. The Buddha encountered disease and decay only when he left the protection of his palace, but we see it every day, on the streets, in our families, at work. Hospitals are part of all our lives, as visitors or patients or employees. Anxiety about bodily health is clearly another driver towards spirituality, again with a self-centred motivation. Bookstore shelves reveal a strong interest in Mind, Body and Spirit, which almost always exceeds the shelf space devoted to religions. Speculation about what, if anything, lies beyond the grave continues. Interest in the paranormal is an industry.

Another anxiety that can be a prompt towards spirituality rather than religion is concern about the future. Rationalists may huff and puff, but horoscopy carries on unabated, whether it be in the small two- or three-line fit-all zodiac entries in some daily newspapers or magazines, or expensive personalized interviews including more intricate and detailed readings of what the stars hold in store. Clairvoyance continues to fascinate. If the future can be 'seen', does that mean that it is already fixed? Predestination as a doctrine in Christianity has long been out of favour, but fatalism outside Christianity is not extinct or even endangered. Soldiers in combat may reassure themselves that they will be OK unless the bullet has 'their name' on and that, either way, there is no point in worrying. It is easy to sneer. But underlying all this are latent beliefs, hopes and fears.

Some of the beliefs are openly fatalistic: 'When you've got to go, you've got to go.' Some are based on the need for reassurance. 'Touch wood' must be one of the earliest examples of secularization of belief. It was originally done by stroking the bark of living trees to placate the tree spirits. But the custom or the words retain an enduring half-magic spell of protection we still invoke, post-pagan believer and post-modern atheist alike. Some submerged beliefs may be half-hearted: 'I don't think there is Anyone out there, but here goes just in case . . .' But the focus of these submerged beliefs and practices remains the self. Protecting the self was the purpose of ancient magic. It proves an enduring preoccupation. It is about safeguarding, comforting, reassuring Me. R. Osmond in *Changing Christian Culture* reports a survey undertaken by the Gallup Organization that seems to accord a high score to spirituality: 58 per cent of respondents thought that life has a meaningful pattern, compared to 30 per cent who see it as a chance series of events and 11 per cent who see it as a mixture. Faced with the proposition 'Life has no purpose or meaning', only 3 per cent agreed strongly and a further 3 per cent tended to agree; 17 per cent disagreed and 69 per cent disagreed strongly. Perhaps this means that the heart continues to run in defiance of the post-modern mind.

Another reason why the spiritual eludes definition is that it means different things to different people. Religions, as corporate and – in terms of rites and rituals – visible enterprises, are less diffusely perceived. Schleiermacher was prepared to offer a definition of the soul, or, as we might prefer to say, the human spirit. For him its existence lies between two opposing impulses, the striving to establish oneself as an individual versus the dread fear to stand alone against the Whole. True religion, to him, is sense and taste for the Infinite. The spirit is not only 'the seat of religion' but its nearest world. Every moment of conscious insight is a spiritual revelation. The heart of religion lies in intuition and feeling. The Deity is only one kind of religious intuition. 'I do not accept the position, "No God, no religion."' The imagination is the highest activity of humankind. 'Your imagination creates the world, and you could have no God without the world.'[15] This comes near to merging what we call spirituality with a reinterpreted view of religion, which would in turn come nearer to including mass or group spiritualities as a form of religion. As we have seen in the case of Diana, these include beliefs that go beyond the secular.

It has already been noted that when the word is used in some contexts, 'spiritual' could merely be a synonym for 'aesthetic'. One might add that if the spiritual could be described entirely in secular language (e.g. in terms of aestheticism) it might mean the end of religion and a victory for secularism. But this is not the case, for two compelling reasons. The first is that, as we have seen, the spiritual can certainly be described but never defined comprehensively in any formula that entirely contains it. The second is that it is quite clear that popular spirituality extends well beyond the secular. However vague such belief might be, it does not concede that the world can be explained by reason alone. Quite the opposite. Popular spirituality is struggling to come to terms with the failure of reason and as such it is a major alternative and rival both to post-modernity and to religious fundamentalism. What it may lack in intellectual credentials it makes up for in endurance. What it lacks in polish it compensates for in sincerity. (The same is in fact true for fundamentalism, which can be seen as another alternative in the face of the failure of reason.)

We tend to think of British religious diversity as being most evident in such cities as Birmingham, Bradford and Cardiff, in which we can find Buddhists, Christians, Hindus, Jews, Muslims, Sikhs etc. But an equally compelling way of illustrating English and British attitudes to religion while taking account of spirituality can be found in a consideration of the town of Glastonbury in Somerset. Set on the once water-covered Somerset Levels and marked by its island Tor with ruined church tower visible for miles, Glastonbury is in no sense a typical English town. Its pop festival is a well-known national event, but it is the way in which heritage religion, living Christianity and other religions and spiritualities co-exist there that makes it a good case study for our purpose. The point of examining Glastonbury is that it contains in a blatant way what is present but more often latent in other towns, cities and villages. It is illustrative, without being typical.

Glastonbury has a long history. When the Somerset Levels were largely under water, before the Roman conquest, a community of lake-dwellers existed near the present site until their destruction by the Celtic Belgae tribe around 50 BC. Legend identified Glastonbury with Avalon, the burial place of King Arthur, and also told that Joseph of Arimathea travelled there with the boy Jesus in the missing years unrecorded in the Gospels. After the resurrection Joseph was said to have returned with the Holy Grail. The Glastonbury Thorn, actually a hawthorn bush, is part of this legend, despite its destruction by Cromwell's men and again by twentieth-century vandals. It sprouted, legend says, where the exhausted Joseph threw his staff on the ground when he reached Glastonbury.

The Abbey itself was a seventh-century Celtic foundation, restored as a Saxon monastery by King Ina around 708. It flourished under Abbot Dunstan (c. 909–88), who restored the whole of English monastic life and went on to become Archbishop of Canterbury. At the time of the dissolution of the monasteries in 1539 the last abbot, Richard Whiting, was hanged from the tower of the church on the Tor for his refusal to yield to the king as head of the church and to allow the nationalization of the abbey. The abbey ruins survive, including a stunningly preserved monastic kitchen. The abbey church is still used occasionally for diocesan pilgrimages and open-air worship. All this could be called heritage religion. Rather like the 'heritage rolling stock' used by some train operating companies, it has echoes of the past and is quaint and rather clapped out. It is a mixture of folk memory, history, legend, conflict, principle and prejudice. It is part of 'our' story by virtue of our being British, though not necessarily 'our' personal story, as we may be British Hindus or British humanists. We can disown the story, but 'heritage religion' is still strongly in evidence. Religious architectural evidences still shape the landscape. The British visit their cathedrals and pay admission charges, albeit as tourists rather than pilgrims.

But Christianity in Glastonbury did not die with Whiting and the spoliation of the Abbey in 1539. It was transformed through changed times into the present Christian institutions in the town. The town has its own churches which reflect the history of English Christianity: St John's (Church of England, fifteenth century), St

Benedict's (Church of England, sixteenth century), the Roman Catholic Church of Our Lady (nineteenth century), the United Reformed (formerly Congregational, built 1814), the Methodist, the Mid-Somerset Community Church and the New Life Family Church (both twentieth century). Unlike heritage religion, which is about birthright one may opt out of, this Christianity has to be opted into. We are not part of it by virtue of being British, since as individuals we may be committed Muslims or atheists or Rastafarians or just too busy to bother with religious choices.

Alongside institutional Christianity there is a riot of New Age and alternative-spirituality shops and practices all along Glastonbury High Street and in the little alleys leading off it. Here one can buy divining rods, crystals, spells from white witches – even cannabis – or go for counselling, group therapy or a Tarot reading. There are crystal healers, astrologers, Shiatsu masseuses, vegan experts, regression therapists, devotees of the Goddess, Berachah colour healers, life-path readers, Reiki practitioners, Feng Shui experts, Egyptian dance teachers and a host of others – all in one small country town. In that sense there is no place quite like Glastonbury anywhere in Britain. Totnes in Devon is similar, but not on the scale of Glastonbury. Yet in another sense Glastonbury makes explicit and visible a lot of the implicit and hidden attitudes, longings, fears and feelings that might be found in any town or village in the UK. These are sometimes known as implicit religion or folk religion or diffusive religion or popular superstition. Nor is there a neat divorce between the Christian and the pagan or alternative spiritualities. Some Christians will use Reiki or talk to clairvoyants. Some pagans may draw strength from aspects of the Glastonbury Christian legend. In any fully rational or secular or post-modern society, all this would have disappeared. But it coexists in a honky-tonk and rakish way – and it shows no sign of disappearing. That is why Glastonbury should be taken into account just as much as Leicester or London in any discussion of the religious and spiritual culture of the UK or its plural society. Glastonbury is a mixture of heritage Christianity, living institutional Christianity, other religions and alternative spiritualities.

'Melting snowmen': national identity, religion and spirituality

'Mae cenedl ag iddi dreftadaeth gref a chefndir hanesyddol yn araf ymbebygu i ddyn eira'n toddi. Mae'r het yn araf gwrdd â'r llawr . . .' ('Nations with strong heritage and historical backgrounds are becoming "melting snowmen". Each and every year the hat is getting closer to the ground . . .') Thus Huw Tudur, addressing the Welsh teachers' union UCAC. He recalled Welsh rugby star Carwyn James, who said that 'without memories, we [the Welsh] don't have a nation'. The effect of this idea on Tudur was profound. As a Key Stage 2 classroom teacher, he was convinced that without memories a nation may die and its language disappear. Education, he argued, is tasked with passing 'memories' on to children, to teach them who they are. Language – in his case, Welsh – is not only a means of expression, but has history and culture intrinsically attached to it. William Morgan's translation of the Bible into Welsh (1588) actually saved the language. Perhaps in England, language has become secularized and lost its associations with history and culture, although as B. Moynihan in *If God Spare My Life: William Tyndale, the English Bible and Sir Thomas More* (2002) indicates, Tyndale's English translation of the Bible (1525) was dynamite precisely because it linked with English history and culture and demolished ecclesiastical control of a Latin sacred text. This change is a largely forgotten part of English cultural heritage: a classic case of memory being lost. The project to revive the Cornish language, even though the last native speaker died in 1777, is further evidence of the way in which language and culture and memory intertwine.

'Britain', as it is now understood, is less than 300 years old, although the ancient Britons (i.e. the Celts, including the Welsh) were pushed to the west by the invading Anglo-Saxons who became the English. Historically Britain can be regarded as the first English empire, one residual imperial effect being that many of the English regard Englishness and Britishness as identical, imperiously ignoring the other constituent nations of the UK. The debate about British national identity, including national 'character', can be traced from the 1880s. Many commentators (e.g. Weight and Beach [eds.], *The Right to Belong*) have held since that time that in the eighteenth and nineteenth centuries, Protestantism lay at the core of British national identity.[16]

In the late nineteenth century the education system was used to promote 'Britishness', for example by special parades and organized games to mark Empire Day. A whole souvenir industry grew out of Britishness. But a century later, Britishness was in sharp decline.[17] Protestant denominations were also shrinking, even in Wales, the land of the chapels. This shrinkage undermined the established foundation of British identity.[18] Teachers were as reluctant to teach Protestantism in the schools as they were to teach Empire.[19] The UK was established, according to Weight, primarily for the purpose of furthering the quest for Empire. When Empire declined, so did the *raison d'être* for Britain – it may gradually dissolve into its constituent nations under a common Crown and as regions of the EU. The Scots and Welsh maintained their identity to protect themselves against a Britain dominated by the English, but the English correspondingly had less need of theirs.[20]

A strong sense of national identity breeds a strong sense of patriotism. Patriotism is frequently linked with heritage religion. 'Patriotism is not enough' are the once famous words of Edith Cavell (1865–1915), a clergyman's daughter and hospital matron from Swardeston, Norfolk, executed for helping 200 Allied soldiers to escape from Belgium into Holland in the Great War. What she actually said on the eve of her execution, as reported in *The Times* of 23 October 1915, was

> Standing, as I do, in view of God and eternity, I realize that patriotism is not enough. I must have no hatred or bitterness towards anyone.

Her remark is worth quoting in full because the frequently cited shorter version is also secularized. When Cavell faced death her expressed sentiment was entirely consistent with Christian faith. But if patriotism is not enough, is the absence of patriotism 'enough'? Nationalism has been discredited by wars, but without some sort of national pride, national identity can scarcely survive. If England and the UK currently have a reduced attachment to religion they also have a reduced national identity, sense of purpose and pride. Are these connected? Do they relate to the litter and dog excrement adorning urban British streets and the fly-tipping and abandoned cars festooning the countryside? Britain's victory in the Second

World War – impossible without the help of the countries of the British Empire along with Russia and the USA – marked also the realization of the beginning of the end of Empire, as well as resulting in a near-bankrupt home economy. Suez (1956) accelerated this, by highlighting Britain's decline as a world power and its dependence on the USA for the approval of future military adventures. It is possible to interpret the following 60 years of British social and political history as a search for a new and appropriate identity.

The search is not over. The UK is still unclear on the extent to which it is part of Europe. The Channel Tunnel, perhaps because it is not visible, like the 10-mile-long Øresund Bridge linking Denmark with Sweden, does not increase the UK's sense of identity with the European mainland. In culture the UK looks more to the USA than to its European partners. Of course, the UK and the USA share a similar language and some common history, but the 'historic relationship' between them is more trumpeted in the UK than the USA. Cynics wonder whether the UK wishes to retain prestige as a world player by being an unofficial State of the Union. British prime ministers are readily seen to fawn to American presidents in pursuit of this influence.

Are people proud to be English or British? Scotland and Wales have stronger national identities. K. Kumar argues that they have their nationalist political parties, for which the English equivalent is the Conservative Party – the English national party. The Last Night of the Proms can for some be a genuinely emotive occasion. But on the whole the British do not hang flags outside their houses, like many people in the USA. The nearest they get is to place very modest Union or national badges on their vehicle licensing plates. English flags appear mainly during World Cup international football tournaments. The first mail-order Union Jack flags complete with flagpoles appeared in 2004 (price £80), but with a coy warning that purchasers should check for planning permission with their local council first. The British do not sing songs invoking God's blessing on the UK equivalent to 'God Bless America', nor do they display pictures of the reigning monarch in their homes. The British national anthem is more often respectfully listened to than sung. Its second verse is virtually unknown. Cecil Spring-Rice (1859–1918) wrote words set to music by Gustav Holst:

I vow to thee, my country, all earthly things above,
Entire and whole and perfect, the service of my love,
The love that asks no question, the love that stands the test,
That lays upon the altar the bravest and the best . . .

This hymn disappeared from most hymn books after millions of 'the bravest and the best' were laid upon the altar of the First World War and butchered. Its sentiment was discredited. This was not prevented by Spring-Rice's stirring second verse about 'another country' for which Christians hope. Bishop Lowe of Hulme has argued recently that the hymn is actually heretical because it puts country above God, with 'echoes of 1930s nationalism in Germany and some of the nastier aspects of right wing republicanism in the US'.[21]

A change in in the nature of national heroes occurred in the same period. A good example of this is Cecil Rhodes (1853–1902). In the days of Empire, Rhodes was seen as a role model for growing children. He was a vicar's son, successful entrepreneur, adventurer, man of action, friend of General Gordon, prime minister of Cape Colony, who defended and extended the Empire – for example acquiring Rhodesia (Zimbabwe) – and solved the Matabele rebellion. With the passage of time and the development of a more multicultural outlook, all this looked suspect, aggressively male, colonialist, even racist – quite unsuitable for children. But what heroes replaced those who, like Rhodes, were dismissed? Mainly pop stars and footballers – mostly male again. One side effect of doting on footballers was the revival of spitting in public, a practice imitated from the on-pitch behaviour of acclaimed professionals.

Despite the monarch's position as head of the Church of England and the fact that Archbishops of Canterbury receive media coverage by virtue of their job, which sanctifies their public pronouncements, there is no national tendency to connect God with Englishness or Britishness. The finest enduring hymn to do that is William Blake's *Jerusalem*: 'And did those feet in ancient time, walk upon England's mountains green?', a probable reference to the Glastonbury legend. This separation of religion from national identity will be thought by many to be the proverbial 'good thing'. But it is interesting to note that many countries in the world, even if their political system separates church or religion from state, do recognize a national religion as part of their national identity. This is not to suggest that somehow the

UK would be improved if this were to happen – such a connection would be inconceivable at present and could never be legislated for or contrived – but to ask whether British national unity is impaired by its absence.

State religion is, of course, frequently controversial. In 1969, the American theologian Reinhold Niebuhr, then in his 77th year, wrote one of his last articles. He called it 'The King's Chapel and the King's Court'. It was an attack on the then US President, Richard Nixon, for holding Sunday services at the White House, starting with one led by Nixon's friend, the famous evangelist Billy Graham, 'a domesticated and tailored leftover from the wild and woolly frontier evangelistic campaigns'.[22] What riled Niebuhr was the Nixon–Graham 'doctrine', as he significantly called it, that all religion was virtuous in guaranteeing public justice and that the religious 'change of heart', much vaunted by Nixon and Graham by means of personal conversion, could cure all people of sin. In other words, the appeal was to the individual. It failed to take account of the dual individual and social character of human selves with all their virtues and vices. Hinting that Martin Luther King might never have been invited to the White House had he lived, Niebuhr equated J. Edgar Hoover, the then director of the FBI, with Amaziah in the Book of Amos. In other words, the taming of religion and by governments is not good for real religion.

But in the UK religion is not only tamed but shrinking. So in what does 'Britishness' reside, since it is clearly not religion? The immediate candidates for Britishness are negative. It would appear to consist in appalling behaviour in Greek holiday resorts, acts of violence by so-called football supporters and scenes of drunkenness outside pubs and clubs every weekend. It might also consist in being xenophobic, expecting everyone abroad to speak English, speaking slowly and in a loud voice to foreigners and demanding fish and chips in restaurants overseas. Honouring Remembrance Day, deep concern for animal suffering but not remotely to the point of stopping factory farming, spectating at football matches (but more of the British actually go to church), queueing in an orderly manner – the list is idiosyncratic and open to objection.

Perhaps Scottish or Welsh or Northern Irish identities are easier to plot than English or British. The English lack national dress, a national dish and a national song. 'Rule, Britannia' is British. Even the English language is so universal that it is not thought of as distinctively English in the way in which the Welsh language is distinctively Welsh. In England the roads are choked, the railways don't work and the two main political parties control the system to shut out the others by denying fairer means of representation, occasionally pausing to worry that the public is cynical about politics. The country seems to survive on a mixture of *Fawlty Towers* and the spirit of Dunkirk. Can the English be nationally proud?

There is a form of patriotism or jingoism under the surface. It can be roused by tabloid newspapers, e.g. in the Falklands War in 1982. This war was the UK's 'fault', since British military intelligence had warned of an impending Argentinian invasion. The Thatcher government chose to ignore this. The one defending British ship was withdrawn on cost-cutting grounds, a supreme irony in view of the later costs of the war. Despite this, patriotic fervour rallied in support of war to recapture the Falklands and South Georgia, islands few except philatelists had heard of before the invasion. Dictatorships taking over small islands perhaps stir the British myth of support for the underdog. But jingoism is not aroused in all situations. The 2003 Iraq War did not witness mass patriotic fervour but quite the opposite, in the biggest anti-war demonstrations in British history.

The UK at present can be characterized as a hedonistic, materialistic society with a great emphasis on individualism that entails the moral autonomy of the individual: do whatever you like as long as it isn't illegal or you don't get caught. Such a society will not have strong national values in any department, for it is at the opposite end of the spectrum to a totalitarian state, in which the individual has no rights. At the individualistic end of the spectrum the state is either ignored or resented, as it impinges on the individual's financial and personal freedom. The state exists merely for what individuals can get out of it – benefits, both financial and less tangible. Some aspects of British life, such as binge drinking among young people, have almost an air of conformity about them: like going to university now, drinking to excess is a rite of passage. But mostly, life is up to 'Me'. Joining organizations, except those that directly promote 'my' interest, such as fitness clubs, has become rather outmoded. Life is fundamentally about satisfying my wishes, my ambitions and my desires, and meeting my personal targets. It is fundamentalist individualism rather than fundamentalist religion. 'Why should I?' appears an unanswerable question when 'I' don't want to do something. The despairing answer of parents and others, when reason fails, 'Because I say so', has no currency in an anti-authoritarian culture. If something is 'boring', and fails to captivate my immediate interest or give me rapid pleasure, why should I bother with it?

Fast food is a symbol of the instant gratification we have come to expect in other areas of life. The self is treated as if it were the focal point of a 'Me-centred' universe, whose planets revolve around 'my' pleasure. 'The self is believed to be at the core of the information universe of cyberspace, choosing, communicating, controlling . . . God-like control is bestowed upon mortals by the power of computers and the grace of VR . . . a sense of limitlessness, of ecstasy, is available in cyberspace.'[23] Regular nightclubbing and sessions at the gymnasium make more sense in this worldview than churchgoing. Even the word 'service', much used by churches, rings strange in a culture in which 'services' are places for toilet stops and refreshment on motorways or something one has done to the car periodically.

Is this 'Me culture' Britain's real 'religion' and national identity? The ubiquitous mobile phone symbolically allows 'Me' to remain at the centre wherever I am and whatever I am doing. 'I' can be in touch with whom I want, when I want and where (in terms of my location at the time) I choose. The subliminal question has become utilitarian: 'What has religion done for *me*?' or 'Do I *need* religion?' rather than 'What do I make of religious truth claims?' or 'What happens to "Me" at and after death?' Religions will not thrive easily in this climate, because they promote either the non-self (Buddhism) or God as their centre point rather than 'Me'. The Osmond survey tends to corroborate this. Faced with 'The main purpose in life is to gain enjoyment from it', 36 per cent of atheist respondents strongly agreed, compared to 18 per cent of agnostic respondents and 14 per cent of Christian.

Should God prefer spiritual fruits to religious nuts as the chapter title suggests? We have seen that the assumptions imposed on the mind by British and European culture disadvantage religions, whereas spiritualities are tacitly approved, provided they help 'Me'. Secular spiritualities – those associated with no religion, no supernatural beliefs, no acknowledgement of the numinous or the Mystery of Life – rapidly run into conceptual difficulty. It is perhaps better to see these sorts of spirituality as aesthetics. Popular spiritualities are emphatically not secular. They are underpinned by all sorts of beliefs and values, even though these are not necessarily those of institutional religions. It follows, then, that spirituality cannot replace religion, because the two are distinct but inter-related. Spiritualities emphasize practice and *seeking* over beliefs and values and, to the outsider at least, religions emphasize beliefs and values and *finding* over practice. This might explain why some religious believers have only a tenuous adherence to their religious institution. They might find a more spiritual form of their religion preferable. This is not a specifically Christian problem, but can also be found in Judaism and some other religions. Popular spiritualities challenge the secularization hypothesis. Only those with closed minds could object to the possibility that, if the strength and fascination of spiritualities and 'personal journey' could unite with the worldviews and narratives of religions, both 'heritage' and 'living', then the religious and spiritual story of Europe would enter a new and dynamically different chapter. But the words are carefully chosen. This is possibility, no more. Such an attitudinal change would necessitate a major shift in how we educate people, along with the views of religions and spiritualities that education is transmitting. To the role of education in this transmission process we must now turn.

5

Education or Catastrophe?

———•◦•———

Human history becomes more and more a race between education and catastrophe.

(H. G. Wells, *Outline of History*,
1920, Volume 2, Chapter 41)

But what if education is the catastrophe? Education has become very much a process that is taken for granted on the part of those involved in it, whether as students, teachers or ancillary workers. Public debate about education frequently focuses on finance, e.g. for universities or their students, or value for money, in matters such as whether inspection reveals that individual schools are efficient. But education is much more than a financial black hole. Not only has education the power to shape minds, but it cannot avoid so doing: by virtue of what it includes and what it omits; by virtue of the real as opposed to the nominal or official emphases during the process; through the ethos of a school or college that values or undervalues particular attitudes or behaviour.

In more recent times, notably since 1988, frequent and sometimes clumsy interference by politicians tinkering with the education process has introduced a situation of almost continuous change. I once examined a PhD in the course of which the part-time and luckless student had had seven supervisors. Not all of these had been competent in the field in which she was working, but nevertheless each had left their mark on the final thesis. They meant well. But the result was a mess that took considerable disentangling. The same is true for the national education system. The spasms of change to which the system has been subjected have been disorienting for those within it. One secondary-school teacher's working life might already span all these changes: the reorganization of schools into the comprehensive system, the rise and fall of CSE examinations, the introduction of GCSE examinations, a national curriculum, and mixed-ability teaching. In addition there are Standard Assessment Tasks (SATs), the change to AS and A2 from A levels, the rise of vocational qualifications, detailed legislation for child protection, Special Educational Needs (SEN) codes, national strategies for literacy and numeracy, the devolution of budgeting to school level, more frequent inspection, school league tables and the rising tide of paperwork.

That list is not exhaustive, so if the teaching force is suffering from burn-out and drop-out, we should not be surprised. While workers in some other fields, notably staff in the health service, can justifiably make similar claims, this does not excuse the treatment British front-line education professionals receive. Considering the way in which a minority of pupils is allowed by society to behave in schools, treating these professionals with disdain, gross disrespect, occasionally violence, we should not be surprised when young teachers drop out within a few years because they claim to 'want a life'. The notion that within the teacher's normal work routines there is time to read, to reflect, to focus on the real purposes and aims of education, is risible.

Of course, teaching will always be hard work whether it is in the reception class or the university, and changes in education are inevitable in a fast-changing society. Some of the changes made by politicians in education have been necessary, judicious, timely and helpful. A moratorium on change would be technically impossible and philosophically undesirable. But the problems with the way in which Britain has handled its educational change have been three-fold. First, changes have rarely been properly financed – the UK has a tradition of parsimony in education that stretches back at least 150 years. Second, the pace of change has been too fast to ensure quality. Third, all the changes have consisted in tinkering or tampering; there has been no coherent vision for education. Put another way, this third problem might be symbolized by the increasing power of secretaries of state for education over curriculum, schools and universities – even pre-school nurseries – since 1988. That ensures that education remains a subject either for pragmatic action or party politics or both. There is no philosophy, no consensual national policy, about what education is for. The situation is Kafka-esque. Thousands of people are tending and maintaining a vast machine and trying to make it respond to the dictates of government, but nobody has an overview of the whole machine or can say what it is for or what the end product really is or should be.

We have seen in Chapter 1 how, for politicians preoccupied with value for money, targets and 'raising standards' to keep their political opponents at bay, and for education professionals exhaustedly and reactively preoccupied with meeting these targets, the values of the system and the process itself remain immune from scrutiny. If this huge and disparate education system were, albeit in an unplanned, unofficial, undirected and undeclared way, suppressing a religious or spiritual approach to life, or the possibility that education in common with the spiritual life might be conceived as a journey, would anyone notice? We are concerned with what lies at the centre of the system – its core value or values. What is it all for? The Polo metaphor reappears aptly (see p. 61). Education has no centre.

To find a serious and profound UK debate on education we have to go back to 1943. In that year Queen Victoria's last surviving child, Princess Beatrice, was still alive. Her mother had come to the throne in 1837. There was a sense of continuity with the past and its values, though shaken by the Great War and fading, to disappear altogether after the Second World War. Much of Britain's already dilapidated school building stock had deteriorated further through neglect during the war years or from bombing. R. A. 'Rab' Butler was President of the Board of Education, then a low-status job, in the wartime coalition government. William Temple, theologian and one-time headteacher, was Archbishop of Canterbury and therefore had a seat in the House of Lords. London was still being bombed. Although the tide of the war was turning in Britain's favour, it was not clear when it would end. Butler, without Prime Minister Churchill's support, wanted to create a comprehensive settlement for educational reconstruction that could be put in place after the war. It was daring even to contemplate such a plan while a world war was in full swing. The churches wanted to see 'Christian education' prominent in this post-war plan, conceived explicitly as an antidote to the techniques of Nazi-dominated countries that had used their school curricula and youth organizations to manipulate young minds. The three Anglican archbishops (Canterbury, York, Wales) in 1941 issued a statement in which they interpreted the war as a sort of crusade pitching Christian and democratic values against Nazi neo-pagan values. Churchill himself spoke of the war as a defence of Christian civilization. The emerging horrors of Auschwitz and the other death camps made this view entirely plausible. It was out of the cauldron of war and the concomitant requirement to think about what mattered most that this debate about the role and place of education emerged. Jack Priestley puts it tersely:

> The British only think seriously about their children and the future at such times as they are suddenly aware there may not be a future to which to look forward.[1]

Only a year before this whole process had begun, Britain had come undeniably close to losing the war on three occasions (Dunkirk and the Battle of Britain during 1940 and the Battle of the Atlantic during the period June 1940 to March 1941).

'Religious education', then conceived of as religious instruction (the classroom subject) plus school worship, was seen as central to realizing the core aim of Christian education. RI was for the first time to become universal in schools, though still subject to the time-honoured parental withdrawal clause. A more ecumenical spirit had brought some conciliation in the bitter denominational disputes that had characterized education settlements in the past.[2] The White Paper's proposals were comprehensive and coherent. A deep and wide-ranging debate took place in both Houses of Parliament, to which the Hansard record amply testifies. Introducing the White Paper to the House of Lords, the Earl of Selborne could say for the government:

> We have now traced the future career of His Majesty's subjects from the day when they first toddle into a nursery school to the day when they emerge as university graduates or are continuing adult education in middle age . . .[3]

Lord Addison referred to the 'calamities' which had arisen in some other countries through the misuse of education. Lord Teviot stated that 'the nations who have struck down religion have become the curse of the world. They have brought this great tragedy [i.e. the war] upon us.' Temple was clearer still about what had to be learned from the European experience:

All education must of its very nature be either religious or atheistic. It cannot be neutral. That is impossible. Neutrality in religion is atheism. It is the same thing. It means, in fact, that if you leave God out, it does not matter whether you think He is there or not. You cannot, therefore, merely have neutral education to which you append religious instruction, as one subject taken alongside arithmetic, geography and the rest. It will never have real value unless it is felt to pervade the education as a whole ... The aim should be to secure that the whole life of the school is conducted as part of the training, not only of citizens, but of Christian citizens.[4]

Noting that the country as a whole had a very small proportion of churchgoers, Lord Clwyd expressed the hope that 'the thoughts of men are widened by education' and that education can help people to realize 'the full meaning and content of religion'. The Earl of Glasgow insisted that

There is something wrong with our education today which has nothing to do with large classes, lack of teachers and perhaps an over-loaded syllabus ... Mere technical efficiency is not enough. The nation must have a soul. Our children must be taught the difference between right and wrong ...[5]

The Bishop of Derby noted the danger in any system of state education of 'totalitarianism and excess of bureaucratic control' and the dangers inherent in the politicization of education.

Reading these debates in full more than 60 years on leaves two abiding impressions. One is that they have not been surpassed in the UK in terms of a non-partisan attempt to make legislation reflect a philosophy of education and take account of the nation's 'soul'. Second is that although the religious map of the UK has since changed, so that it is no longer possible to equate religious education with Christian education, or to conceive of 'Christian education' as appropriate for all the UK's children, many of the insights of this debate remain prophetic. The best education will inevitably have clear core values that are transparent and consensual. If these are limited to the secular so as not to offend particular religious or atheistic groups, then, as Temple said, they are in practice anti-religious since they leave religion out. That teaches by implication that religious values are either not 'true' or not important or both. The difficult formula for UK education has to be to ensure that spiritual and religious values are at the core. This would in fact democratically reflect the 2001 census in terms of religion. But the core values that take account of a religiously plural society must not become 'anti-non-religious'. By that ungainly phrase is meant the shutting out of the option of a secular life stance in the same way that the restriction of core values to the secular shuts out the religious. A secular life stance is not 'wrong' morally, intellectually or socially. It should not be evicted from the core. It has the same right to exist as religious stances for living. But it must not be allowed the privilege, for which it sometimes criticizes religious life stances, of dominating the core. For that sort of dominance it has no mandate. Nor must it be allowed the falsehood of posing as value neutral. Attempts by some proponents of an entirely secular core to shout down religious or spiritual claims for core position on the alleged grounds that only 8 per cent of the nation attend a place of worship regularly are entirely misplaced. The religious and spiritual map of Britain is far more complex than that.

The attempt to exclude no one's sincerely held religious, spiritual or secularist view on life from the core of educational values may promote the adoption of secular core values on the basis that they constitute a common denominator, to which religious and secular people alike can subscribe. It is argued that since secularists find difficulty with religious language and thought forms but the religious use secular language and thought forms for at least some of the time, they could unite on the secular in the interests of harmony. This is no solution. For in subscribing in this way, religious people would be surrendering their own core values as secondary. They would have reneged on the uniqueness of a religious view of life and the language in which it expresses itself. Liberal Christianity has done this repeatedly in the past in its desire to mate with the spirit of the age, as has been demonstrated previously (see p. 62).

This readiness to abandon religious principle accounts for some Muslim critique of a multicultural society as westerners understand it. The foundation multicultural values in such a society are not religious but secular. What is strange is not that this type of multiculturalism is found unacceptable by Islam, but that it has been found acceptable by western liberal Christianity. Adopting an alternative approach is not a call for denominational or inter-religious strife, or for a religious war of words, or for intolerance or for the promotion of one religion or secular stance above others in state legislation. It is simply a call to re-examine fundamental values and to face difficult questions. When too many things are swept under the carpet of 'toleration' in order to avoid searching debate and self-scrutiny, fanatical religion and fanatical irreligion can erupt in their frustration at the inanity of avoiding truth claims in the interest of a superficial harmony. Can this sort of 'avoidance toleration' engender terrorism? It could contribute if it stifles debate and is based on unchallenged but highly contentious secular values.

It would be difficult enough to delineate core religious and spiritual values for education if Britain had a longstanding tradition of quality debate about education. But as we have seen, this is not the case. The university curriculum for initial teacher training, even the monitoring of university research endeavour, is now controlled by external agencies. For teacher training these include the Teacher Training Agency, the Qualifications and Curriculum Authority, the Department for Education and whatever its most recent suffix is (it has been at different times Science, Employment and Skills), government legislation and frequent and time-consuming Ofsted inspections. Two-thirds of the graduate teacher-training one-year course is spent in the school classroom. What time is left for philosophy? We should be working from core values to curriculum, but in Britain the process has been reversed. We have to deduce values from the curriculum. Thus the values behind British education at present remain largely unknown, unscrutinized and undebated. It is time to examine how the religious element is actually treated in the system at present.

What the curriculum does to RE

The national unease over what to do about religion (is it the illness or the cure?) meant that when the national curriculum was introduced in the 1988 Education Reform Act, religious education was relegated to a place outside it. The national curriculum plus RE was defined as the 'Basic Curriculum', whatever that was intended to convey. The locally agreed syllabus for RE remained legally binding, but it was hard to see RE as having parity with other subjects when its syllabus was derived differently and when it was not part of the national testing procedures which were set up at that time. Later recommendations on time allocation awarded only 5 per cent of curriculum time to RE. Compare maths, which occupies a baronial position within the curriculum, reflecting the widespread and largely unchallenged 'belief' that maths is 'important' and 'useful'. This was challenged by a mathematician, Professor David Burghes, in 2003.[6] The revision of 14–19 curriculum to re-emphasize 'vocational' education (itself a significant word) may preoccupy education even further with the empirical and verifiable.

But the attitude towards RE in any nation's curriculum only reflects the attitude towards religion(s) in the host culture. It is sometimes easier to see this process in relation to a different culture. The Kingdom of Jordan provides a brief case study. If we consider the Arab world, Islamic education plays a crucial role in developing the values and morals of Islamic societies globally. The term 'Islamic education' conveys a dual meaning. It is an overall approach to education based on Islamic principles and therefore affecting all curriculum areas. It is also a discrete curriculum subject throughout the Arab Muslim world and known by different terms: Islamic education (*al-trbi'ah al-islam'eh*), Islamic studies (*al-derasat al-islam'eh*) and religious education (*al-trbi'ah adene'eh*). Islamic education is a high priority within the Jordanian curriculum, as Islam is the official religion. Sunni Muslims make up 95.8 per cent of the population. Christianity is the main minority religion, approximately 2.5 per cent of the population. Muslim–Christian relations are good.

Islam is presented under several branches of Islamic knowledge including the study of the Holy Qur'an and of the al-Hadith. In the past, family, mosque and society shared the task. Systematic teaching is now left mainly to the school.[7] If their role is diminishing, the role of the school in the transmission of Islamic values increases. Islamic education is therefore awarded 10 per cent of curriculum time and is taught by traditional methods from a text produced centrally by the Ministry of Education for each year group. It would not be at all unfair to characterize the process as Islamic nurture. In line with this concept, teachers of the subject are expected to be good Muslims and act as role models for the children.

British society is a much more complex one religiously to mirror in its RE. Until the early 1960s religious education and Christian education were viewed as largely synonymous. That meant that the syllabus was largely biblical – it was not thought strange to study a living religion solely through its scriptures – and there was concern about the difficulty of recruiting enough Christian teachers to do the job. This concern featured in the 1943 parliamentary debates. RE at that time was therefore in intention liberal Christian nurture, not so much to 'win souls for Christ' as to nurture children in the heritage religion of their country, allowing them the freedom to discuss and question. They were encouraged to become mature, adult members of the Christian faith, without any strong-arm attempt at compulsion. But a series of studies in the 1960s showed that the current teaching was ineffective and unpopular with children.[8] These studies were hailed at the time as revolutionary. In fact they merely revived, confirmed and updated evidence that dated back to the 1930s and had been forgotten.[9]

The result was what was called at the time a 'revolution in RE', also referred to as the 'New RE'. This was enthusiastically, occasionally fanatically, anti-confessional. It did not assume a Christian base as the only option for sensible living and it accepted the claims of secular humanism to be considered as a life stance. In the 1970s, partly as a result of the work of Ninian Smart at the University of Lancaster and the realization that some large cities were by then visibly multifaith cities, world religions entered the British RE curriculum, taught from a mainly phenomenological base. The Birmingham 1975 agreed syllabus for RE is a landmark in this transition period and became controversial only by virtue of its intention to include, in optional units, communism and humanism as stances for living. There was no fuss because it intended to teach Islam, Sikhism, Hinduism, etc. In the sense that these world religions were also British religions, at least in the cities, RE from the mid-1970s did reflect a changed society. But in teaching world religions, early attempts to found teaching on 'neutrality' were naïve and were eventually abandoned as impossible. The castigation of the old methods as 'confessional,' i.e. teaching which assumed or was intended to promote a religious (in this case Christian) base, led to RE teachers falling over backwards to demonstrate to pupils that they were not trying to indoctrinate them. By doing this, they may have unwittingly provided an alternative sub-text, namely that religious truth claims are controversial and divisive and should be avoided in classroom teaching aimed at promoting tolerance and multiculturalism.

When this happened, it did all religions a big disservice, as truth claims lie at their heart. It also had the effect of sanitizing religions in the classroom. Members of different world religions simply became the nice people next door, who were really 'just the same' as 'us' except that they might wear different clothes or eat different food. Hinduism, for example, was easily reduced to saris and samosas. The notion that religions change lives – hence might change the life of the student – or that religions might motivate people was played down. The 21st-century discovery that a tiny number of the religious people next door might be terrorists exploded what was left of this inane 'we are all really the same' view.

Michael Grimmitt, in a widely influential book, *What Can I Do in RE?* (1973), argued that the justification for RE must be educational rather than religious. He saw its potential to develop the child's cognitive perspective and to aid personal development. Grimmitt added that RE can be used to teach what are now known as thinking skills and that its aim should be empathetic: children should 'step into the shoes' of what a believer feels. He wrote:

> If RE teachers could adopt the attitude of a shopkeeper with wares in his window which he is anxious for customers to examine, appreciate and even 'try on' but not feel under any obligation to buy, then many of the educational problems connected with RE would disappear.[10]

The shopkeeper provided a very vivid model to help UK religious educators in the 1970s to present themselves as distinct from catechists and to justify their position, especially within the curriculum of non-church schools. This was important during a time of declining church attendance and the wider apparent decline of the Christian base of UK society. By presenting itself as a non-confessional and not necessarily Christian activity, UK RE ensured its survival outside church schools. Grimmitt's 'shopkeeper' kept the 'business' afloat in a rapidly changing market.

In this way, British RE unknowingly equipped itself to outlive the decline of the churches from the 1960s onwards. For some commentators this was a betrayal of its responsibilities. Liberal Christian educators are said to have 'sold the pass' for Christian education when it should and could have been held.[11] But one cannot imagine all UK schools today teaching Christianity *as true* in RE, at the same time finding teachers willing to do it and children willing to listen, leaving the other religions to withdraw their children or argue for apartheid in religious teaching. In 1986 Trevor Cooling attacked Grimmitt's shopkeeper analogy, noting that it wrongly implies that all the 'wares' are equally valid.[12] He pointed out that there may be other items under the counter that are being deliberately withheld from the customer, e.g. fundamentalist 'brands' of religion. He might also have added that shopkeepers frequently steer or manipulate customers towards the wares they want to promote.

What RE failed to do, however, through all these years, was to address British culture as it was. It did not take account of the popular spiritualities, the Christianity of the 71.6 per cent, secular life stances – which under the microscope reveal just as many intellectual problems as their religious counterparts. Over the decades from the 1960s, perhaps out of sheer embarrassment about its subject matter – religion – RE entered a number of dangerous curriculum liaisons to make itself look 'relevant'. A few schools tinkered with the subject's title and tried 'Life Studies', 'Ethics' or the notorious 'Humanities'. In this latter, usually in association with history and geography, RE appeared, sometimes in separate modules, sometimes in integrated studies. Thus in primary school 'Hums' work on 'Our Village', the RE component was often the parish church, treated historically and geographically (dating, monuments, building construction, measurements, etc.) apparently anything other than religiously. Other religious or spiritual presences in the village, perhaps the Methodist Chapel, the Jehovah's Witnesses' Kingdom Hall and the yoga club would be ignored, as would beliefs. The humanities focus would be on the human, not on the question of God. But religions deal with the possibility of God. This meant that 'Hums' was implicitly anti-RE, as God was ignored. Epistemologically, RE has far more in common with the creative arts than with history and geography, but the 'Hums' grouping was very common and survives in a few time-warp '70s' schools. In many 'integrated' courses RE frequently disintegrated and disappeared.

Multicultural education appears to be a natural ally for RE, which has the potential to contribute to it powerfully. A cross-curricular approach rather than a timetabled subject, multicultural education is another example of the improvisation approach that has a long tradition in UK education. It was seen to be desirable by people in the field and so it evolved in a rather uncoordinated way until a major report, *Education for All*, better known as the Swann report, appeared in 1985. Before 1985 multiculturalism in education had been implicitly secular and suspicious of religious imperialism, including the years of Christian dominance of RE, and tended to see religion as a source of social division rather than integration. A pre-Swann book for teachers, although demanding that 'all [text] books should be scrutinized for racial, religious and sexist bias', makes no mention of RE on its list of curriculum subjects which could contribute to multicultural education.[13] Although religious confessionalism was attacked, a different sort of confessionalism seemed to be at work in some aspects of multiculturalism: it called for commitment, attacks on racism and a purging of unsuitable materials. These are, of course, defensible aims, but it is interesting to note how one sort of confessionalism becomes anathema while another is acceptable.

One study of multicultural education listed its key fields as developmental education, environmental education, human-rights education, anti-racist education, equal-opportunities education and peace education.[14] Religion did not figure. Again, it is hard not to conclude that before Swann, multicultural educators were either ignorant about RE or had been programmed with a sort of secular suspicion of religions. Swann, which did not like faith schools, more than affirmed the importance of RE as an agent in multicultural education – RE was hailed as crucial in the process. Of course, to be perceived as a key agent for multiculturalism was not always beneficial to RE, for this perception could lead to a tendency to avoid divisive issues and truth claims, concentrating instead on harmony and mutual understanding as educational objectives. There was a danger that the study of religions might be seen not as a particularly beneficial or absorbing ends in itself, but simply as a vehicle to engender a more tolerant society.

Another common curriculum bedfellow of RE was personal and social education (PSE), originally 'moral education', and sometimes known as personal, social and health education (PSHE). The syllabus content of PSHE is secular, as are its curriculum assumptions. This did not prevent RE in some schools merging with it in Key Stage 4 (ages 14 to 16), especially in non-examination courses. No writers on PSHE theory willingly admitted its unpopularity with many children at classroom level or with some of the reluctant teachers who were drafted in to teach it because they needed their timetable filling up. So in some schools the uninterested teacher led the bored child and RE was roped in, usually losing the 'R' in its subject content in the process. Fortunately, by the mid-1990s RE and PSHE were being seen as separate and RE could recover its own identity. But in schools where PSHE swallowed the RE experience of the child it is important to analyse what was happening. Following the study of religion up to the age of 13, this swing in the syllabus took the child into a study of moral issues. The subliminal message is clear. When you are a young adult, you leave religion behind and go into 'morality'. You graduate from the religious to the secular. Religion is kids' stuff.

No sooner had the PSHE stranglehold on some RE courses relaxed than 'citizenship' arrived on the scene. This was British 'patch and mend' at its best, or worst. No great educational or philosophical theory and no curriculum Grand Plan lay behind it. The politicians were running scared. There was increasing voter apathy, especially among the young. The political parties were experiencing continuously falling membership just like the churches. Moreover, individualism seemed so rampant that society began to look as if it might be disintegrating. There was much publicity at the time and subsequently for Prime Minister Margaret Thatcher's infamous assertion, 'There is no such thing as society. There are individual men and women, and there are families.'[15] The politicians did not examine themselves and what they were offering as one possible cause of this malaise. They were not offering proportional representation to make every vote count, but instead a very antique system claiming to be democratic and trumpeting its place in the 'mother of parliaments'. The main parties were not offering any political options that were opposed to increasing European political integration until the 2005 referendum. While arguing the need for migrant workers to fill jobs, at the same time they were publicizing housing shortages, road overfill and the need to build on green belt. There had been no solution by Labour or Conservative governments to transport problems known about long before Richard Beeching was appointed (in 1963) – by politicians – to slash the national rail network by a third, a decision everybody knew was short-sighted at the time. So there was plenty in the politicians' statement of account for them collectively to answer for.

Instead, with all the certainty of those who have been to school and therefore 'know about' education, they came up with citizenship on the national curriculum to redeem the apathy of the young towards the political process. For Key Stage 3, the QCA scheme of work included human rights, political structures and process, the media, sport, and links with history, geography and RE. In the case of RE, the link identified was the study of conflict. We shall see whether citizenship brings voters flocking back to the polls. It was introduced with no study of its past in British education. Some of its proponents seem to believe it was a new curriculum subject invented by government in 2002. In fact citizenship went back well into the nineteenth century, to Thomas Arnold's scheme to produce 'Christians and gentlemen' at Rugby in 1828. Citizenship had appeared in the British curriculum in the 1930s and again in the 1950s. Nobody bothered to learn from what had gone before.

In preparing for its reincarnation in 2002, there was typically no debate about what the 'city' was into which teachers were to be busily inducting young citizens. Was it England? Or the UK? Or Europe? Or the world? Or Plato's city? Or Augustine's 'city of God'? All this illustrates once again that the damaging view of curriculum held by British politicians is mechanistic and instrumental. You use it to do things, regulate things or change things. As the Hebrew Bible observes, 'where there is no vision, the people perish' (Proverbs 29.18). A few voices even suggested that outside faith schools, citizenship might replace RE, but this would be problematic for three reasons. First, the content of the two subjects is widely different. Second, citizenship is taught from a secular perspective. Third, RE is about the child's entitlement to know about religions and about a religious way of life as an option. No other subject provides that.

It is a long time since RE could be described as under threat, but it is still not a fully accepted member of the national curriculum and is still subject to a parental withdrawal clause redolent of the old 'RI' days. In a democracy, it is right to offer withdrawal from religious instruction. But religious *education* is different. The withdrawal clause should be extended to all curriculum subjects or abolished. The latter is unlikely to happen, as it would easily be portrayed as a human-rights issue and the secularists would thunder against it in their media pulpits. RE as a curriculum subject remains a minority provision, even with ongoing moves towards centralization of the RE curriculum. Some schools continue to flout the legal requirements for provision, despite Ofsted inspections.[16] There seems to be a correlation between support for RE in a school from the senior management team and whether the subject is properly timetabled, staffed and resourced. There is still a serious shortage of specialist teachers for RE. A headteacher who is a religious maniac can be prevented from inflicting this obsession on pupils, but a headteacher with a 'down' on religion can starve RE of staffing and resources very effectively. Yet examination entries for religious studies are rising at every level (see pp. 80f.), so it is also important not to get a persecution complex for RE. A recent study detailed government interference with syllabuses carefully proposed by professionals and government determination to make the subject content-driven rather than skills-driven. The writer lamented the reduced role of the subject in post-14 education and raised the serious question whether it would even survive on the curriculum map. The subject of this book was not RE but geography (Walford, *Geography in British Schools*).

What RE sometimes does to religions

Slicing religions

For many years after Goldman's *Religious Thinking From Childhood to Adolescence* (1964), and in some schools now, thematic teaching was widely used in RE in the first three key stages (pupil ages 5 to 13+) as a way of presenting religions. So, for example, units of work appeared on sacred writings or pilgrimage or places of worship or rites of passage or founders. In each unit a number of world religions were given an appearance, so that for example the Hajj, Lourdes, Amritsar, Canterbury and Jerusalem might all appear in a unit on pilgrimage. Although it was widely espoused in the profession and has defenders still, this was damaging for RE, for four principal reasons. First, it is conceptual nonsense to imagine that one might understand a religion by seeing one slice of it alongside slices of other religions, any more than one might understand a pig by examining a piece of bacon. Second, it encouraged unintentionally a dangerous concept of equivalence. That is, that the Christian Bible is the equivalent of the Qur'an to Muslims, the Guru Granth Sahib for Sikhs, or the Upanishads for Hindus. Or in a similar way, that a rabbi is a 'Jewish vicar', a gurdwara is a 'Sikh church', etc. Third, the themes selected were always phenomenological and nearly always secular. Units rarely appeared on God, revelation, sin, mysticism or prayer. Fourth, at pupil level it created confusion. 'Isn't a rabbi a Hindu priest, Miss?' Undeterred, the slicing of religions by RE syllabuses continued into Key Stages 4 and 5 (ages 14 to 18+) in GCSE, AS and A2 examinations. Here the Bible was reduced to a textbook of ethics from which students were required to learn selective quotes from passages to address syllabus work on war, euthanasia, divorce or sexual ethics. Passages were given neither context nor those culture clues needed for students to interpret them. Jesus was reduced to an ethical teacher who apparently died not by crucifixion but by the death of a thousand cuts as his sayings were cut and pasted into syllabuses.

A trip to the museum, Jurassic Park or the zoo?

There is a danger that RE sometimes makes the study of religion look like a museum visit, a study of what people used to believe. Visits to empty places of worship can sometimes reinforce that impression, because the people are missing – and the place is often cold. Children do not readily appreciate that not all congregations in any religion can afford seven-day heating of their premises just for occasional and usually non-paying visitors. Jurassic Park and the zoo are variants on the museum theme. The religions are alive, but they contain rare and unusual animals, endangered species, which we do not meet in everyday situations. In other words, religions are not normal – they are sometimes distinctly odd. We approach them at our peril, in case they 'get' us. They have been known to devour people. Staring at the exhibits in the zoo is also a strange experience. We are 'free'; the animals are not. We are in some ways superior to them. We watch their strange behaviour. We meet them on our terms. We control the encounter. They are not allowed too near us. They sometimes make sounds we do not understand – liturgical language. In an increasingly secular society like England, the teaching of world religions in RE mainly on a phenomenological basis runs the risk that this is the impression created or reinforced in the mind of children.

RE has sometimes secularized its own subject matter
It could reasonably be expected that among its other functions, RE
would present the case for religious belief within an open context
that recognizes the child's freedom to choose a religious or a secular
set of values and beliefs, or not to choose anything particular at all.
Indeed, because of the widespread ignorance about religions one
might expect that RE would be scrupulous in presenting the religious point of view fairly. This has not always happened, however.
The worst examples have arisen in lessons involving teachers who
genuinely believed that they were delivering RE. No better example
of this can be found than in the treatment of the Joseph/Yusuf narrative, a 'golden oldie' of Key Stage 2 (junior school) RE. The long
tradition of using the Joseph narrative in Key Stage 2 RE contrasts
with a long but rather pallid tradition of training and support for
primary-school RE itself, where most teachers are non-specialists. It
has become common practice for Key Stage 2 teachers to tell the
Joseph story, rather than use textual study in their own preparation
or with the class. They frequently go on to develop visual display via
murals or topic books produced by the children. They have then
'done' Joseph. Or have they?

Joseph appears in the Hebrew Bible in Genesis 37 and 39—50.
Christians, in adopting the Hebrew Bible as their 'Old Testament',
took the Joseph narrative into their scriptures. In the Gospel of
Matthew (c. 85 AD), which uses typology as a method, the Joseph of
Genesis is seen as a 'type' for Mary's fiancé or husband Joseph, who
is also credited with receiving special revelation from God via
angels and dreams, and going 'down' to Egypt (Matthew 1, 2). As
Yusuf, Joseph appears in the Qur'an. Sura 12 is named after him. It
starts mysteriously with the Arabic letters A, L, R, one of a number
of Suras to start with letters whose meaning is held to be known by
Allah alone. While in Judaism and Christianity he is something of a
seer and a sage, in Islam Yusuf is accorded the very special status of
a prophet, one in a series of prophets beginning with Prophet Adam
and ending with Prophet Muhammad. Thus for Jews, Christians and
Muslims, Joseph/Yusuf is a significant figure. On a global basis and
within three religions, many millions of religious believers are
familiar with the Joseph/Yusuf narrative in one of its two main scriptural forms.

There is agreement as well as divergence between these scriptural narratives. The most important common feature is that the central agent is 'the Lord'/God/Allah. God directs the events and determines the outcomes. In Genesis the climax is 45.8: 'So it was not you [the brothers] who sent me here, but God; he has made me a father to Pharaoh and lord of all his house and ruler over all the land of Egypt.' Allah appears 45 times in Sura 12 as 'Allah', 14 as 'rab', 20 as 'We' and 12 times under names and adjectives such as 'the Merciful'. There are 91 references in all. In S12.100 Allah is the one who grants the original vision and makes it come true. Yusuf submits to his will and is protected. God is the real 'hero' of the narratives. However, less moral aspects of Joseph appear in the Hebrew Bible narrative, e.g. his calculated impoverishment of the Egyptian population (47.13–26). Here Joseph becomes an oppressor who enslaves the Egyptian people, a remarkable destiny for an outsider who was rescued by God from his own afflictions. This part of the Hebrew Bible narrative is no part of the Qur'an. More surprisingly, it is virtually unknown in RE. One commentator puts it like this:

> Joseph, who was delivered by God out of his own destitution and slavery, quickly forgot where he had come from and . . . turned his power . . . into an instrument for the oppression of others . . . Stories like this one are told again and again in the Bible . . . However, children seldom realize that the Bible tells this kind of story.[18]

Hull's own view is that children never realize that the Bible is about the deliverance of the oppressed by God because they are never told. A rich world has chosen to omit this bit of the story in the telling in order to sanitize the narrative. It could equally be that those teachers who choose to tell it don't bother to read the Genesis text, instead transmitting what they remember being transmitted to them.

In addition, however, to the Josephs of Judaism and Christianity and the Yusuf of Islam, there is a fourth Joseph. In western culture a secular version of the Joseph narrative arose in the twentieth century, possibly in RE lessons. At junior-school classroom level the narrative was being told without any mention of God, as a secular adventure story. But merely because the narrative originates in the Bible, it was still being hailed as RE. This version of the story acquired considerable influence and status, increased or perhaps reflected by the continuing success and international appeal of the musical *Joseph and the Amazing Technicolor Dreamcoat*, by Tim Rice and Andrew Lloyd Webber. In this show, Joseph is something of an opportunist, possessing integrity, a person who strikes lucky and makes the best of his 'breaks' without abusing others. He is the epitome of a secular westerner in the late twentieth century. The themes, although distantly biblical ('I have been promised a land of my own'), caught a mood of assertive individualism which was sweeping Europe and continues to dominate western society, notably that 'Any dream will do', the significant lyric of the finale. For the Joseph/Yusuf of the Bible and the Qur'an, any dream will simply not do, since dreams and visions are one way of mediating direct messages from 'the Lord'/God/Allah. But *Technicolor Dreamcoat* reduced Joseph/Yusuf to the subject of a highly entertaining, memorable, religion-less pop oratorio, in tune with an increasingly secular society. The Prologue includes a terse statement of western relativist values:

> But if you think it, want it, dream it, then it's real
> You are what you feel

The musical grew via various versions into its present form, the story of which omits 'the Lord'/God/Allah completely. For many western children the Joseph story is no more than an entertaining tale because only this version has been presented to them, via the musical or via RE lessons which have edited God out of the telling. If there is a moral or spiritual dimension, the child is left to impose it. This is a fundamental distortion and misrepresentation of the biblical narrative, but as in a good conjuring trick, you can't see what's not there. So the secular Joseph has attained world status just as real as that of the Joseph/Yusuf of the Hebrew and Christian Bibles and the Qur'an.

The damage to RE from the 'fourth Joseph'

There is nothing 'wrong' with a secular Joseph any more than there is anything 'wrong' with a secular view of the world. But it becomes harmful in the context of education if it is presented as the *only* view of the world, or as the *only* version of the Joseph story that pupils encounter. The rise of an entirely secular Joseph within an education process that claims to be open represents the sort of censoring of religious narrative against which the Biblos research project warned.[19] It suppresses a truth claim in all three religions' scriptures, that 'the Lord'/God/Allah is the supreme agent behind human history and is active in the world. When children encounter only the secular Joseph narrative they are in no position to accept or reject the truth claims of the religious narratives, or to choose religious belief. They are being offered no choice at all, not even a basic understanding of the originating narratives. In many schools, recordings or videos of the musical became a teaching device offering memorable and enjoyable lyrics and music and even the option of a school production. But if teachers stop there, they provide only one Joseph, without even acknowledging the existence of the others. What is indoctrination if not the reduction of choice to one, i.e. no choice? This is a clear example of the fact that western RE, when badly done, can secularize religious material in the classroom, robbing it of its central theme and distorting the originating tradition. Such a presentation should more accurately be described as anti-RE because it subverts the objectives of RE to present religious traditions faithfully and accurately and to allow for pupil choice. Removed from their originating culture and presented without clues to that culture, religious stories can be seriously misunderstood.[20] But the Joseph narrative is not the only one to suffer this sort of treatment.

David and Goliath

David and Goliath is another primary-school classic. Yet it can be reduced to a moral story about bullying for use or abuse in personal and social education or in collective worship ('assembly'). It is sometimes presented within the theme of bullying. David stands up for himself against the giant and bully Goliath. The little person stands up to the big person. Don't let yourself be picked on. This is confirmed by pupil 31 in the 2004 Biblos survey: 'no matter how small u are, belive [*sic*] in yourself'. Pupil 177 in the 2003 Biblos survey says that 'David killed Goliath because he wasn't chicken' and that the narrative means 'be courageous and face certain death bravely' (is this advice to David or Goliath?). Presented in this way it appeals to the British cultural concern for the underdog. Pupil 538 endorses this explicitly: 'there is hope for the underdog. Even when the odds are stacked against you, you can still come out on top.' Pupil 32 (2004) on David and 'Guliufe': 'don't hert [*sic*] people because they might actually be nice'. But even a cursory examination of the Hebrew Bible narrative (1 Samuel 17) shows that these themes and values, laudable as they may be, have nothing whatsoever to do with the encounter between David and Goliath. That is, if indeed David encountered him at all, for an alternative version suggests that Goliath was killed by one of David's bodyguards, Elhanan (2 Samuel 21.19), unless there were two Goliaths.

Using a good translation and commentary we can understand that Goliath, an infantryman, possibly of Anatolian genealogy, protectively armoured except for his forehead, was using the latest technology, iron weaponry. This was superior to the Israelites' bronze weapons. He challenges the Israelite army to produce a champion to fight. Bullying, the picking on a weak person by a stronger, is simply not in the frame. Goliath demands to fight *anybody*. One can say, therefore, that he demonstrates a sort of confident or brash courage, backed up by 'state of the art' armour and weapons. He is a good soldier. The Israelites in contrast were explicitly afraid (verse 24) and by implication not good soldiers. But Goliath's error is specific: he 'defies the armies of the Living God' (26, repeated for emphasis in 36). Who can expect to prevail against the armies of the Living God? So Goliath exhibits at least misjudgement or perhaps misplaced belief in his own gods (43) or monstrous arrogance, in taking on the Living God. David believes that this God, 'the God of the armies of Israel' (45), will be instrumental in Goliath's defeat (37). The death of Goliath is forecast to be a sign 'that there is a God in Israel' (46). Goliath may be armed with the latest technology, but David is armed with 'the name of the Lord of hosts' (45). In other words, as so often in the Hebrew Bible, the rather scary hero of this narrative from a literary point of view is God. It is in God's power that David wins and in this power he can only win. When he acts without it he can only lose, as happens later (2 Samuel 12.1–23). With this as the context, there was no contest.

It might be rather unpalatable in our culture to present God in this way, but we have no right to excise narrative and rewrite previous cultures. Similarly, whatever the teacher's personal view, she must be faithful to the narrative and can preface what she tells the class by words such as 'in the narrative, God . . .', or 'David believed that God . . .' An atheist or agnostic teacher can still present religious narrative fairly and retain their integrity. But where secularization of this narrative in primary school occurs, it does real damage to religious understanding. This is because at the end of all the moralizing about bullying and standing up for oneself, another generation thinks that they 'know' a biblical narrative that they do not in fact know or understand at all.

Learning from religion or engaging with religions?

Unfortunately that is not the end of the matter. The secularization of religious material extends to other cases. The parable of the Good Samaritan is frequently reduced to an ethical exhortation to help those in need. The Prodigal Son is reduced to a secular ethical exhortation to forgive. Jesus is reduced to an ethical teacher who urges humankind to be more loving. In such a presentation one is left wondering why anybody bothered to kill him. In the Biblos questionnaire, pupils themselves provided further examples of this trend. They were asked to name one passage from the Bible, briefly to describe it, and then to answer the question, 'What do you think this story/passage might mean for people today?' The meaning of the Genesis creation narratives, according to Pupil 752, is 'work, but you should take time to rest and appreciate life'. Feeding the five thousand means 'don't take things for granted and share things' (Pupil 758). The Good Samaritan cropped up in race relations: 'just because someone from one country is bad doesn't mean they all are' (Pupil 692). The 'Pronical [*sic*] Son' means 'you'll always be wanted' (Pupil 36). It could be that these examples take their tone from the wording of the question, which did not ask pupils to describe what the passage might mean for Jews or Christians today, but more vaguely 'for people'. But this is no different from the widely used Attainment Target 2 for RE, Learning from Religion. Nobody has satisfactorily explained precisely what pupils are expected to 'learn from' religion. Probably this attainment target was conceived as a counter-balance to Target 1, Learning about Religions, which in itself could be rather arid. Learning from Religion is not intended to be proselytizing, but to encourage pupils to take out some value for themselves from the religion they are studying. It is – accidentally – a clear steer towards the secular. Nor is this secularization confined to biblical narrative. In some RE lessons, Martin Luther King has been taught as a civil-rights activist, without attention to the Christian mainspring that was his motivation. Another instance is teaching which, while acknowledging, say, the Qur'an to be in Muslim belief divine revelation, in practice presents it as a product of Islam, as if without Islam to promote it, there would not be a Qur'an. The possibility of God, of divine revelation – that this book might actually be a communication from God that could change human lives – is played down. Instead pupils are urged to treat each copy with great respect rather than read it (in a paraphrase): encounter it physically, but not in its content or truth claims.

If RE has sometimes secularized its own content, it has also fallen victim to political correctness. Historically great strides were made to integrate members of different religions into UK education (Birmingham 1975 agreed syllabus onwards), to bring parents on board and to give faith-community leaders a voice in RE. The RE Council, a voluntary body, has representation reflecting Britain's major religions. All this is laudable, since any aims for education as a whole, other than the narrowly utilitarian, must include attempts to create knowledge, understanding and tolerance between people of very divergent lifestyles and views. But even in this process, political correctness has appeared. In RE textbooks it has become *de rigueur* to write 'pbuh' (peace be upon him) after the name of Muhammad. This is a statement of deep respect accorded to Muhammad by Muslims, who do not of course worship him. But to refer to Jesus as Christ or Lord in a classroom textbook would be howled down as insensitive to non-Christians or arcane or 'confessional', teaching that assumed or intended religious commitment on the part of the child. For the same reason BC and AD have been sacrificed to BCE and CE. Some RE textbooks still put vowels into the Jewish sacred unpronounceable name of G-d, or even into YHWH. Why is the playing field not level? What do these inconsistencies in 'correctness' in textbooks reveal about attitudes to Christianity or Judaism or Islam?

When biblical or other religious narratives are taught badly to the young – the Virgin Birth, Noah, Joseph, etc. – they may have to be 're-learned' later on. That is possible only if teachers can see what has happened and know how to move on. But the alternative is bleaker: these narratives may be discarded in later childhood, along with religion, as incredible. Many adults can testify that their childhood experiences of RE were disappointing. For some they may even have been damaging, as we have seen. Even in a world-religions context, RE does not always appear interesting or to reach the parts that other subjects do not reach. 'Learning about' in RE will always be important, but not as an end in itself. It is a means to an end. 'Engaging with religions and other life stances' would be far better as a single attainment target for RE. RE should induct children in an informed way into what is a debate, extend their options, dispel ignorance and misconception, reveal hidden assumptions, allowing them to see whether and how they have been 'programmed' with a worldview they might not wish to own and what other options are available. If children are to develop spiritually they will do it reflectively, with awareness of divergence and difference and with wonder at 'mystery'. Enhancing the capacity of children to 'theologize', far from taking them back to an obsolete way of learning, may be seen as the main task for RE in the early twenty-first century. Alongside this will be the capacity to include the spiritual in RE, without at the same time being confessional. This is a tightrope walk for the teacher, but it is possible.

'O Lord, make haste to help us': school worship

Collective worship, a term used in the 1988 Education Reform Act, is more often known by its user-friendly historic nickname 'assemblies'. If any activity connected with education looks on paper like religious indoctrination, this has to be it. It is daily, compulsory (subject to parental withdrawal rights), collective *worship*. It is important to note that the law does not define this event as corporate worship, worship by a body or corpus of believers. It is collective worship: a more random collection of people than a corpus is involved in this act.

School worship is an orphan in curriculum terms. Outside faith schools, nobody on the staff 'owns' it. Collective worship is frequently not resourced from the school budget. No teachers are trained to lead it. RE teachers long ago severed the connection that had been thought in 1944 intrinsically to link them with school worship: religious theory in the classroom, religious practice in the hall. Worship appears on few, if any, PGCE training courses for teachers. It is rare to see in-service training available for experienced teachers. Two web sites of material to help leaders, promoted by the Culham Institute, Oxford, and by the SPCK, are exceptions.

They get many 'hits'. Secondary-school heads of year are presumed competent to lead worship on their appointment. Primary headteachers are expected to function in the same way, as if an enchantment falls upon them on the day of their appointment, which mystically prepares them for this role. Add all this to the British unease about religion and it is easy to see two things. One is that the occasion has transmuted in many schools, especially secondary schools, into a moral rather than a religious or even spiritual event. Often a moral homily by a senior teacher is given, sometimes boringly. No one should be surprised in the light of all this that worship in schools lacks friends and that it can easily be perceived as obsolete and unviable. The surprising thing in terms of the starvation of priority, attention, staff training, resourcing and decent accommodation for the event itself over the many decades to which it has been subjected is that school worship has survived into the twenty-first century.

Yet worship is often the only experience to bring the whole school or year group together. It can be very enjoyable in primary schools, even if those memories are later overlaid by memories of secondary-school apathy and boredom. The obvious solution to all these difficulties is to remove worship from the school's obligations (apart from faith schools), or to make it voluntary. Another solution would be to accept and legitimize the transmutation of the event into a moral occasion and to conduct what the British Humanist Association calls a shared-values assembly, in which there is no pretence at worship. Reducing the number of 'acts of worship', something many teachers would like to do in order to achieve better quality than the 'daily' requirement of the law permits, is less attractive than it appears at first sight. Teaching is so hectic that any time gained from reducing collective worship would not, realistically, be invested in better planning for those acts of worship that remained. The time would go into marking, preparation for inspection, parent interviews, seeing individual children, or the many other tasks teachers face daily. Moreover, the ethical and educational difficulties raised by collective worship would not be solved simply by reducing the number of events. These difficulties arise from the nature of the events, not their quantity. The other two options carry equal problems. Make school worship optional and we simply further privatize religion. Abolish it and another area of the child's life is made secular. Is there any way out of this dilemma?

Collective worship produces what can be identified as a triangle of tension. The three points on the triangle are the requirements of the law, the aspirations and needs of schools as communities of education and the need to protect the integrity of teachers and their pupils. In summary: law, education and integrity. In practice it is relatively easy to hold any two of these together in a specific event of worship. To have a place in a school or community of education, collective worship needs to fulfil some educational requirement. One can do something educational that preserves the teachers' and pupils' integrity – but it may not meet the legal requirement. Or one can do something legal that is also educational, but invades the integrity of staff or pupils or both. Holding all three together is much more difficult. The use of periods of silence helps in terms of integrity, for in silence one can meditate, pray to a God or simply daydream. Corporate prayer, on the other hand, compels or coaxes everyone to go through a form of words.

In the years immediately after the 1988 Education Reform Act I suggested to many panic-stricken secondary-school heads, on courses convened under imminent Ofsted inspection of school worship, that they might adapt the BBC Radio 4 'Thought for the Day' as a model (see p. 49). This was suggested not as a model for technique and method, but a model of theory for collective worship. 'Thought for the Day' is presented as a 'thought' or reflection from a position of religious or sometimes humanist commitment. It is not evangelistic in intention, but is intended to provoke its audience to reflection or action or to challenge their own spiritual life in some way. The listeners are a 'collection': some making the car journey to work, others shaving, applying make-up, washing up, getting up, breakfasting; they are of different shades of religious belief or none. They are usually people on the move. Children in collective worship are also people on the move, into or just out of a lesson. They too are of different shades of religious belief or none.

A live event does not have to be as passive as a radio 'Thought'. In collective worship children do not have to be reduced to listeners. Interactive approaches can be adopted. Children can be involved in making or reacting to the presentation. If the reluctance to discuss collective worship were removed – teachers rarely explain to children what it might be for or how it could be used, or 'train' their children on how to use silence pauses creatively – the children might see more value in the exercise. But perhaps lack of confidence among teachers that they should be engaging in this sort of activity communicates unease to the children. In faith schools the issue is somewhat easier because Jewish, Muslim, Christian or denominational Quaker, Seventh Day Adventist, Roman Catholic or other worship relating to the foundation status of the school is possible. But the triangle of tension referred to above is a reminder that in any community of education, the integrity of the pupils and staff must still be preserved and what happens ought to be in some way educational as well as legal. Amazing as it seems, worship has the potential to be de-indoctrinatory because it offers a window into a different 'take' on life and is capable of looking at the whole. The rest of the curriculum looks at pieces, segments, compartments, 'subjects'. The rest of the child's school experience is fragmented into maths sets or tutor groups or lunchtime clubs or the group of friends on the school bus. Those schools that are making links between collective worship and the cross-curricular theme of spiritual development are making most progress here, as the act of collective worship is being integrated into the life of the school and not left outside, the orphan in the cold.

Over many years a tradition of stodgy assembly anthologies sold reliably, helping teachers short of time to find a reading to use when leading school worship. A brief survey of this anthology provision revealed that in the 1950s the paradigms in the books for 'senior assemblies' were nearly all male, and that they were provided as Christian examples of courage, self-sacrifice, service to others or missionary endeavour.[21] Grace Darling, Gladys Aylward, Lawrence Oates, Wilfred Grenfell and, in an exception to this Christian establishment gallery, Rabindranath Tagore featured in the anthologies of that time. These replaced anthologies starring an earlier generation of fearless British Christian men such as General Charles 'Chinese' Gordon, who had given their lives in the service of Empire. It looked as if in order to be featured in school worship, one had to have been dead for at least ten years but not more than a hundred. But by the 1990s most human exemplars in anthologies had given way to themes: being human, global village, rights and responsibilities, ecology. It was significant that we had done with heroes.

In this we return inescapably to Britishness. As we have seen, the

British seem to have done with heroes. Pop stars and football players are the nearest we have to heroes – royalty, politicians and successful business people don't fit the bill and explorers nowadays seem more wacky than heroic. But pop stars and football players are endlessly exposed in the popular press for aspects of their personal lives we would not, if the tabloid allegations are true, wish to commend to our children. Violence, racism, and exploitation or actual abuse of women are just some of them. Perhaps Princess Diana was symbolically the last British hero. Human enough to be 'one of us' and cultivated as 'the people's princess', she took initiatives in welfare work with the problems caused by landmines, the social isolation of Aids patients and many other charitable causes. But now Diana is dead. Perhaps the national grief at her death was a realization that it created a void in national life. Having on the surface dispensed with God, and made religion a matter for embarrassment and discarded heroes, the British have nothing left to worship. Could this be the real problem facing school worship – the problem is not intrinsically with worship but with the British?

We have seen that British education resembles the Tin Man in L. Frank Baum's *The Wonderful Wizard of Oz* (1900). It operates effectively and credibly within certain parameters, but it lacks a heart. Consequently it lacks wholeness, cohesion and sense of purpose. We cannot say that it has a religious or spiritual centre or purpose, or indeed any self-evident purpose at all. In that sense education is pragmatically secular, secular by default. By proposing no great religious or even spiritual theme or purpose, it produces graduates at every level from nursery school to university who do not see – as a result of passing through education – that life itself might own or could be given a religious or spiritual theme or purpose. The only implicit purpose for our education system is to acquire qualifications to help 'Me' to achieve what I want to achieve, whether a GCSE in Spanish, a WEA flower-arranging class, or a PhD in quantum mechanics. Education has been reduced to the acquisition of a product.

Yet if we propose helping people to find meaning in their journey through space and time, as members of their locality, their area, their country, their continent, their planet, their universe, they need more than a spirit of acquisitiveness. We should be identifying a spiritual or religious purpose for education that could unite all the subjects of the curriculum. If it could not, in a post-modern age, offer a universal and unifying purpose for education, it might still offer the equipment from which a personal view might be constructed. In so far as we were talking about the micro-narrative of individual lives and not one, single, shared meta-narrative, we might even find favour with post-modern thinking. The challenge would then be to translate this aim into practice in such a way that it would be neither as distant nor as dead as the current mission statements of some big organizations. Such statements in theory give their employees unity and a sense of purpose but are frequently derided in the workplace. As we have seen, for the religious person the statement proposed above still does not go far enough. For many religions, to grow in the knowledge and love of God is the 'purpose' of human life. Education for them would matter in so far as it enhanced such a purpose. But this way of conceiving the matter would pose serious problems for non-theists. This will be considered further in our final chapter.

So much for a religious or spiritual purpose for education as a whole. But what about religion within the curriculum, mainly (but not entirely) in RE? We have seen that the ambivalence of the British towards religion is reflected in the status of RE. Like a big dog one might want in an emergency, one likes it around, but it goes into a kennel outside the main house in case it bites us. This is the position of RE outside the national curriculum. Moreover, as we have shown above, RE if badly taught can damage religious understanding and even carry out a transmission of secular values – secular indoctrination. Because God has been removed from the narrative the 'doctrine' indoctrinating the children is that God is unreal or absent. Instead get on with life and try to help each other. There is nothing 'wrong' with this secular humanism as a carefully considered life stance, but when it is used as a filter to censor religious narrative, it becomes dangerous. In this situation it damages pupils and also the religious tradition or narrative being presented.

Yet despite some bad teaching, without RE as a curriculum subject the claims of religion would never be heard in the lives of many pupils. Their ignorance of religious matters would be unchecked. They would lose a basic human right to the option of a religious or spiritual way of life. The English teacher is thrilled if her pupils choose to go to see a Shakespeare play of their own free will. The

RE teacher is worried about indoctrination if her pupils rush off to a place of worship. But who is worried if the pupils drift into a respectful agnosticism born not from conviction but simply from a mixture of pluralist relativism ('religions can't all be right') and a failure to see religions as something more than lists of beliefs? 'It doesn't matter what you believe, as long as you lead a good life.' How sanitized can you get?

6

Fighting a Vapour?: Secularization, Religion, Education and the Future

———◆◆◆———

> You cannot pit yourself against a vapour! . . . It is there – in eyes
> and nose and throat one smartingly feels it, but, when you close
> your hand upon it, it is there no more.
> (W. E. Sangster, *Methodism Can Be Born Again*, 1938, p. 24)

Sangster's words on the difficulty of combating secularization were
remarkably prophetic for 1938, although J. H. Oldham had seen secularization as a threat as early as 1931.[1] They both saw that if one
tries somehow to 'manage' secularization, the exercise is akin to
attempting to plait fog. At present we cannot even 'manage' education, despite a plethora of education-management courses, because
we do not know to what destination we wish to take it. If we can't
manage education, do we have any chance with secularization?

What do we really want our children to learn and value?

Beneath this question lurks a more fundamental one, namely: who
are 'we'? Whose voices should be heard and how should the process
of deciding what a nation's children should learn begin? One answer
is that there is no 'we', only diverse and sometimes conflicting
voices. There are even four countries, England, Wales, Scotland and
Northern Ireland. Are there also four nations? If so, this still omits
the Channel Islands and the Isle of Man, which are distinctive con-
stitutionally and culturally. It is easy to forget that the UK has at least
four native languages, quite apart from Urdu, Punjabi, Hindi, the
other languages spoken by British Asians and other ethnic groups,
and the surviving Norman-French patois of Jersey. So 'we' are a
wide-ranging group, diverse ethnically, linguistically, culturally, over

many centuries. The 2001 religious census suggests that 'we' *en masse* are supportive of religious values, particularly of what must be presumed to be a very broadly conceived Christianity. 'We' include and embrace various world religions and also a significant minority who are clear that they are entirely non-religious.

The support for a broad Christianity may be more passive than active, but it is inclination, not disinclination. 'We' – in this case the intellectuals among 'us' – must stop pretending to be 'post-Christian', without at the same time reintroducing the undemonstrable claim that Britain is a Christian country. This is an Alice in Wonderland situation. We were never a Christian country in the first place, but we can hardly be a post-Christian country while 71.6 per cent of the population claim to support Christianity. It is vital to make more sense of that 71.6 per cent adherence to Christianity by exploring the many popular spiritualities. The statistics of church attendance remind us that 'we' are by no means as supportive of institutional Christianity. For this reason alone, trying to march people up the old church path would be a non-starter. But so would be turning our collective back on Christianity altogether.

Much of our present education process is devoted to knowledge, understanding (sometimes) and skills. Skills are prized because they are held to be transferable into different situations. Knowledge is impossible to keep up with and tends to go out of date. In most situations, understanding and making sense of what we know matters at least as much as what we know. Knowledge without understanding is suitable for the pub quiz or TV game show, but does not equip for life. It is only in a static society that knowledge is vitally important for its own sake and older people are valued as repositories of knowledge and relevant experience, because they live in a slowly changing world. But now that *Nineteen Eighty-Four* and post-modernism have claimed that even the past can be rewritten into whatever we make it, we seem to have collectively lost the desire to seek to understand how we have come to be where we are now. This is especially true of our cultural history.

One thing is notably missing from this education wish list: wisdom. If only our politicians, our journalists, our educators, our famous people were wise . . . Can wisdom be taught? The Hebrew Bible assumes that in some way it can and provides the Book of Proverbs as an example of both principles and maxims. Sirach in the Apocrypha is a sec-

ond example. We find wisdom difficult, because it is classically linked
to God:

> All wisdom is from the Lord,
> And with him it remains forever.
> The sand of the sea, the drops of rain,
> And the days of eternity – who can count them?
> The height of heaven, the breadth of the earth,
> The depth of the abyss and wisdom – who can search them out?
> (Sirach 1.1–4)

Wisdom is also related to emotional intelligence. Truly wise people
are never insensitive brutes in the emotional life; quite the opposite.
But by what higher 'wisdom' have some Europeans dispensed with
the collective wisdom, accumulated over millennia, of the world's
great religions? By what criteria can they be totally ignored or dismissed? That comment is made from a purely human perspective,
for there is also inherent in these religions the possibility of divine
revelation, that God might have spoken or be speaking now. The
'wisdom' that can afford to throw away every religion that has ever
appeared on the face of the earth without so much as a cursory
examination looks more redolent of Babel-like folly.

Atheism has indeed come of age. No European can be unaware of
that. It has a right to be heard and to be treated fairly alongside religions both in society and in education. But it remains a minority
view and it has no right to dominate either the media presentation or
the educational presentation of religion, either by offering a one-
sided view of religious material or by encouraging the deliberate
omission of the religious or spiritual dimension. Of course religious
and spiritual views can legitimately be criticized in education – but
so should atheistic and secularist views. There is a 'right to know'
about religions that must not be repressed. There is a 'right to criti-
cize' that must be extended to critiquing atheism and agnosticism.
The west may have to learn to challenge the strident evangelical
voices of atheist secularists, just as it has learned to challenge or
comfortably dismiss the voices of doorstep religious evangelists who
explain on each periodic six-month visitation that the world is on the
verge of ending. Where secular indoctrination processes and values
are at work they need to be exposed to scrutiny. This should be the

task not just of religious educators but of all educators who consider themselves worthy of the name. Although cultures usually change slowly and mainly as a result of what at the time are imperceptible processes, that does not mean we are doomed to be the hapless victims of particular cultural trends, in this case secularization.

What British religious education needs to do in this situation is not to continue teaching a sort of disembodied world-religions course as it is currently doing, but to engage with the complex cultural realities of religion in Britain, including popular spiritualities. In this context Glastonbury (see pp. 94ff.) is just as much the key as Coventry to understanding the religious and spiritual climate of Britain. It is a world-religions-plus-spiritualities approach that is required of RE, one which at the same time acknowledges the option of atheism as a valid personal response and accepts the cultural responsibility to induct children into heritage religion. Without the latter we would be bringing up a generation of children like visitors to a museum in which none of the exhibits is labelled. No wonder they get bored and want to leave. But religions are much more than museum exhibits. Moreover, the engagement with popular spiritualities should be neither to tame them nor to improve nor to patronize them, but to recognize that they simply reflect where many people are. This is a far nobler cause than to be engaged in secularizing religious material in a specious effort to make it 'relevant', an activity which is actually complicit in the secularization process. The present national attainment targets for RE – learning about religion and learning from religion – should be replaced by the more vigorous single target: engaging with religions and other life stances.

What we want – or ought to want – our children to learn and value as they pass through the education sausage machine is that life is mysterious, diverse and precious. The meaning of life is not, ultimately, sausages. Education should not first and foremost be a production line. Life is a matter for intellectual analysis at the same time as emotional wonder and response, but it is hard to hold the two activities together. Western education has tended to extinguish the latter. Education should also promote respect for oneself, for all other sentient beings (not just selectively for some) and for the planet. This value should not be so much taught as a duty as evoked as a response. Rights should be trumpeted only if they are linked with responsibilities, not promulgated in a dangerous isolation that simply fuels the individual's feeling of self-importance in a Me-centred universe. Education should concern itself with three great human themes that are also biblical themes: destiny, encounter and vulnerability. These themes provide a bridge between some of the great themes of the Bible and the perennial preoccupations of growing children. They also avoid the jargon that religions sometimes spawn. The Bible is about human vulnerability, intensely significant human encounters and the destiny of people and nations. But it is also about the encounter with God, the destiny God wants for the world and, in the Christian story, the vulnerability even of God, as a baby and as a crucified man. Young people are concerned with the encounters they have with adults and each other, with their vulnerability (e.g. first day at school or work, or issues of dating and bullying) and with their destiny (what I want to be and what I want the planet to be). The themes touch all of us and are not the monopoly or possession of either Christian believers or believers in general.

Most of all, education should embrace the possibility of God. That is not the same as embracing the certainty of God, in the face of which one could only instruct students to believe, or to try to compel faith – in other words indoctrinate. Nor is it to teach that God is a 'fact' that cannot be challenged or denied, or that atheism is intellectually shabby or immoral or inferior to theism. But what is happening at present in education and wider British society is tending to eliminate or deny the possibility of God. The central question should not be whether we 'believe in' God (see p. 19), but rather: what does it mean to take God seriously? – incidentally a question that it is perfectly proper for an atheist, in consciously rejecting God, to be called upon to answer. If the tendency to eliminate God from British discourse continues, it will exacerbate a problem for the collective mind of British people. Their feelings will continue to signal the failure of reason and – in some situations – of material values, while their intellects will simply be trained to ignore or to stereotype the claims of religions about God, reducing God to an optional cerebral 'idea' that the individual chooses to adopt or not. This would be akin to programming under-nourished people to recognize food as poison and therefore reject it. If confused and confusing spiritualities have resulted from this situation in the struggle within the British mind, who can be surprised?

The deceptive equation

Religion can be good or bad in its moral outcomes.
Wonderful deeds and terrible atrocities have both been done in the
name of religion.
Humankind should prefer the morally good to the morally evil.
Therefore morality offers more hope than religion.

In this 'equation' lies one part of the secularist case. If this is right,
it is better to dispense with religion and simply abide by the moral.
But this is a flawed argument. In the first place, some would argue
that the third proposal (humankind should prefer the morally good to
the morally evil) historically and culturally stems from religion.
More importantly, all human beings are good and bad morally. The
Zoroastrian analysis of the world as a moral battleground has much
to commend it. In many, perhaps most, human beings there are ten-
dencies both towards goodness and towards badness though one
often predominates over the other. Humankind, in so far as it has a
collective identity, shares this dual tendency too. This is analogous
to 'bad drivers'. Sometimes each of us is a 'bad driver', while some
of us are bad drivers more frequently than others. But Jesus himself
rather surprisingly admonished one enquirer who, flatteringly or
genuinely, addressed him as 'good teacher': 'Why do you call me
good? No one is good but God alone' (Mark 10.17).

For the atheist, morality must always offer more hope than religion, since religion is untrue. For the believer, religion always offers
more hope than mere morality, for religion is true. For the believer,
religion or 'the will of God' provides the reason for moral striving.
So the underlying question should really be not whether morality
offers more hope than religion, but whether the truth claims of religion or those of atheism are sustainable. Whichever way education
decides to 'answer' this question runs the risk of indoctrination. If
education ignores the question – as in the USA – it also commits
indoctrination, by virtue of not providing children with the tools and
skills with which to enter the debate, or teaching them that the question is of no importance. They are then left prey to media impressions of religion or its doorstep vendors or to the unbalanced
preaching from secular pulpits of some journalists. The only role for
education in this apparent impasse, therefore, and one which is truly

'educational' rather than indoctrinatory, is to induct children into the debate. That is, to create both a climate of discussion in which strongly held views are respected and listened to and a climate of information and understanding so that strongly held views, whether theistic or atheistic, are not merely prejudices aired as monologues. For between believers and unbelievers, which group could claim a monopoly of prejudice?

Will secularization prevail?

Across the planet religions are alive and well and constitute a potent force – not necessarily for good – in the lives of billions of people. The power of religions may be morally opaque, but it is no less real for that. To understand humankind on the surface of the planet we have to attend to religions. But as we have seen, in Europe – in the UK especially – religion in general and Christianity in particular have become 'a problem'. This is ironic in a culture that has been shaped by Christianity in its art, architecture, language, literature, legal systems and music. Secularism, the eager promotion of secularization, remains the conscious creed of a minority even among the atheist minority, but many more people appear happy to lead secular lives without being evangelical about it. European history suggests that the pendulum will swing back. But although there is much more residual belief than the size of religious congregations in Britain implies, the pendulum does not yet appear to be moving towards institutional religion. If anything it is still swinging away. The world religions have collectively demonstrated that they can adapt to enormously different cultures and deal with change over long time spans. That is precisely why, sociologically speaking, they became world religions in the first place and not just local or national movements or sects. So we must not don funeral clothes too quickly for the death of religion.

Religions are volatile and unstable, sociologically speaking. Rather like volcanoes they can lie dormant for many years and then erupt very suddenly. We cannot easily imagine an Islamic Europe or even a re-Christianized Europe. But when a handful of Jews believed that God had raised from the dead an obscure Galilean – a man who never had an education, never wrote a book – no one could imagine that he and his God would have billions of followers all over the planet 2,000 years later. When only a few people believed in the message recited by Muhammad, who would have thought that billions would hail him as the 'seal of the prophets' and identify the words that he was given as the words of Allah? The world has already been rewritten, more than once, by religion. So it is possible – probable? – that the tide of secularization will one day be reversed.

Religious revival – do we really want it?

All religions are potentially threatening to political establishments. This is because the religious allegiance of the individual is frequently stronger than national allegiance, and obedience to religion is more compelling than obedience to the state, as a study of the history of more than one religion can testify. Religions can overthrow governments, which is why some Arab countries are fearful of Islamic revolution and try to maintain their hold over their people by savage repression if necessary. Religions can create new allegiances, rewrite cultures, even rewrite themselves in cycles of 're-formation'. So religions are sometimes unstable or even destabilizing forces, not only for individual lives but also socially, politically and culturally. We should not be surprised, therefore, when governments try to tame them, bring them under the arm of the establishment and draw them into conformity with society. The secular powder keg in which people in the UK are currently living is potentially explosive. That is to say, nothing in the present culture is preparing them for the astonishing vitality of religions or the surprises they are capable of delivering. For religions can outlive civilizations themselves. We may currently be enjoying a genteel secular picnic on top of a rumbling religious volcano.

What this means is that if a religious revival were to happen, people would be so unprepared that they could be swept off their feet. In a world of email and the internet, the spread of a new cult and its values could occur faster than any religion previously known. The fashion towards the secular could be quickly forgotten in an eruption of mass piety so frightening and suffocating that those outside it might find themselves under pressure to join the crowd. If this did happen, would it be a new manifestation of an existing religion, or a completely new faith? The possibility of a Muslim Britain has already been canvassed, but it would be unlikely to be Islam in its Arab or Asian cultural wrappings. British history has seen sufficient

Christian revivals to make it impossible to rule Christianity out, despite the current anaemic position of the churches. British culture and history have prepared the ground for Christianity, but then the current almost anti-Christian sentiments among some people would work against that. Could an entirely new religion arise? New religions do arise, explosively, like supernovas, stars and planets. The UK would not need to be its birthplace. In a global village where any one place can rapidly be linked with everywhere else, and virtual reality can transport us anywhere, the geographical starting point is now irrelevant. A new prophet or guru could arise within an existing religion (not in a Muslim understanding of prophecy or Sikh understanding of guru-ship, of course) or to found a new religion.

Is this likely? It is certainly possible, but how probable is it? The truth is that nobody knows. When revivals erupt, historians and sociologists explain clearly and convincingly why they arose in a particular time and place, but spotting them in advance is more difficult. There is no equivalent of the space telescope to enable a prediction of when and where a new religion is going to explode. What we cannot do, however, is to rule out the possibility. Howard Gardner, writing in the entirely different context of analysing human intelligence, notes that 'ours is an era devoid of heroes and bereft of leadership'.[2] He finds leadership within 'domains', people who exercise leadership in business, or the arts, or technology, but notes the desperate lack of leadership in wider society. In each domain, he argues, the leader is recognized by the members of it as possessing an excellence in intelligence in that domain. Outside these specialist domains, there is no automatic way of attracting followers. Then, fascinatingly, Gardner continues, 'a would-be leader must be able to create a story about that society – a persuasive narrative that accounts for his or her place within it and one that can link individuals of different intelligences, domains, and allegiances in a more incorporative enterprise.'[3] Traditionally, this is exactly what founders of religions have done so successfully. Will the new prophet have an MBA? Might this leader also be black and female?

Rethinking the idea of religion

'What Christianity all boils down to is . . .' But do religions have 'essences'? Do they 'boil down' to one-liners and the soundbites so beloved of the media in their treatment of serious or deep topics? Religions offer 'ways of life' rather than creeds. Creeds should perhaps be viewed more casually as attempts to deal cerebrally with deep collective experiences and express them using an economy of words. Instead they have been used as boundary markers to create insiders and outsiders or as sticks with which to belabour the 'unsound' or the heretic. Some people might be more attracted to a creed expressed in music (not words set to music, but music only) or art or dance. Even silence. Perhaps religion needs to learn to loosen up and move away from the old Protestant dependency on verbal expression. That would be cool, or as the French put it, *branché*, not for the sake of being cool, which would actually be gimmicky, but naturally cool. But if there is no such generic entity as 'religion', do we have to translate what we refer to as religions into something different? Comparative religion proves in the end that all religions are not the same and that they do not easily fit into common categories conjured up by westerners. The western tendency to codify and label might have led us into 'defining' religions that are just as indefinable as spiritualities or that have to be understood differently. Are we mathematicizing the mystery by reducing it to formulae? David Jenkins, with scant regard for ecumenical political correctness, is scathing about the monotheistic religions' failure to obey God:

> The Jews have failed to recognize Jesus as the Messiah, the Christians have failed to obey Jesus as the Messiah, and the Muslims have chosen a warrior prophet instead. What that means is that we have all got God, to a great extent, wrong and so we are in danger of becoming one of the greatest threats to the future of the human race rather than God's offer of service to and for the whole human race.[4]

If he is right, not only have we mis-defined religion, but the monotheistic religions have missed their way. Redefining religion, or adjusting the ways in which we think about religions, opens up the possibility of exploring the relationship between religions and spiritualities more easily because it makes religions like spiritualities, in some sense negotiable, rather than leaving them to be perceived as fixed take-it-or-leave-it systems. A dialogue between the two could, presented via the forum of education, help the many people with religious beliefs and spiritual feelings, but who are outside the orbit of institutional religions, to clarify their discourse and deepen their beliefs and values.

Intervening to change the present cultural trend

Cultures inevitably change over time, but can they be changed and shaped by direct intervention? An advert asking people to foster teenagers in *The Big Issue in the North* asked its readers if they 'remember the first time you stayed out all night'.[5] It reminded them that being a teenager involves 'all those hormones flying around, the confused feeling of not being a child, but not quite an adult'. But in reality this is what we in western culture have made our teenagers into and that is the behaviour we have come to expect from them. They are merely conforming to a role expectation, reflected in this advertisement, that they will stay out all night, or be generally difficult.

On Monday 1 September 1828, Thomas Arnold sat down for the first time to teach the sixth form on 'an undignified kitchen chair at the little table' in the Upper Bench classroom at Rugby School, not elevated on the common teacher's dais of the time. Unknown to everyone that morning including himself, his first day in the classroom at Rugby marked the beginning of a new era in English education, one that would be misreported afterwards as the taming and modernizing of a wayward school and the start of the cult of organized games. None of these things was true of Arnold's headship. He was head of Rugby from 1828 until his untimely death in 1842. What he did there was to undertake a radical educational experiment with two aims: to try to produce a truly and not merely nominally Christian community in a school and to try to abolish adolescence. This experiment has never been thoroughly evaluated, but the second aim was not as crazy as it first appears. Adolescence is not a necessary phase of the human condition or genes but a product of culture. For instance, it did not exist in biblical times, since children were married off as soon as they reached puberty. In other words the childhood–adulthood transition was direct. There was no intervening phase. So there is nothing inevitable about adolescence. It is in many ways a western construct caused by delaying full entry into the adult world for up to ten years beyond the maturation of the body. No wonder it is frustrating for those locked into it by their age and the surrounding culture.

Arnold viewed adolescence with loathing. He was well aware of institutionalized bullying and sexual abuse during his own boyhood at Winchester School. He listed six 'evils' of adolescence that might exist in a school. These were: 'direct sensual wickedness', i.e. drunkenness and sexual abuse; 'systematic falsehood', when lying is the accepted practice of the great majority of pupils and tolerated by all of them; 'systematic cruelty' such as bullying, especially of pupils reluctant to join in 'the coarseness and spirit of persecution' all around; 'a spirit of active disobedience' in which all authority is hated and rules deliberately flouted; 'general idleness' where the tone of the school is such as 'to cry down any attempt on the part of any one . . . to shew anything like diligence or a wish to improve himself'. Finally there is the bond of evil, bad friendships, 'by which a boy would regard himself as more bound to his companions in ties of wickedness, than to God or his neighbour in any ties of good'.[6] Although we would express them in different terminology, some of these traits can be found in some British schools today.

Arnold wished to elevate teaching from the training of the intellect to the training of character. For Arnold, education did not *include* spiritual development; its whole aim *was* spiritual development, which he understood as the Christian path to Christ. But if these were visionary aims, there were also practical objectives.[7]

First, he elevated praepostors (prefects) almost to the status of teachers. He treated them as young gentlemen, not as necessary evils in the task of subduing the lower school. The theoretical defence for this practice was that being accorded such responsibility was a training ground for those responsibilities of adult life they would be expected to shoulder on leaving school. He therefore gave them great trust and expected complete loyalty in return:

> When I have confidence in the sixth, there is no post in England for which I would exchange this; but if they do not support me, I must go.

The corollary was that, to the surprise of many observers, the highest offence in Arnold's Rugby was to lie. This was more serious than bullying, theft, fighting or any other offence. When questioned by a praepostor, a boy's word had to be accepted, but woeful would be the punishment if he were later found to be lying. Arnold trusted what his pupils said and there was even comment in the school underworld that there was no point in trying to fool 'the doctor', because he always believed you. Four praepostors were invited to dine with the Arnold family in each week of term time. Arnold wanted his praepostors to possess not only the right behaviour but also the right mind. The seriousness of Rugbeians at Oxford attracted comment, both favourable and unfavourable. Arnold was prepared quietly to expel the worst troublemakers. The fictitious but credible bully Flashman of *Tom Brown's School Days* was characteristically dispatched without ceremony first thing in the morning after his final offence. Arnold was also ready to advise the parents of pupils making no progress to withdraw them, despite the fears of his trustees that numbers – and therefore fee income – in the school would reduce. In fact they rose.

> Till a man learns that the first, second and third duty of the school-master is to get rid of unpromising subjects, a great public school will not be what it might be, and what it ought to be.

Arnold's attempt to abolish adolescence was a qualified failure. What it shows, however, is that rare quality, an educator willing to dare, someone unafraid to challenge the conventions of the time. Today's educators have to be like performing circus dogs jumping through the hoops placed there by their political ringmasters. If Arnold were a head today, he would soon be suspended – but then he fell foul of the press often enough even in his own time and on one occasion was nearly dismissed from Rugby. He would have emphatically endorsed Thomas Merton's aphorism about the spiritual life, 'Do not be one of those who, rather than risk failure, never attempts anything.'[8] Do we really want western adolescence to persist in its present unlovely form? And have we surrendered the belief that education can change things?

Indoctrination

The question we set out to examine was whether a secular indoctrination process is at work in British society and, if so, to what extent education and the media have been complicit. The evidence is complex and at times contradictory. The religious signals are disappearing or being transmuted, like Christmas, into something fundamentally out of alignment with their originating religious or spiritual experience and heritage. If we visit our cathedrals, it is usually as tourists – outsiders looking in – rather than as pilgrims. The idea of institutional religious affiliation or commitment has been erased from the minds of most people, or to put it more accurately, it has never crossed the threshold of their minds in the first place. To the extent that institutional religion and its claims are not considered seriously, or even at all, by the majority of the population (or, less likely, that these claims are so unconvincing as to make no sense to them), we are indeed a secular society. The British mind has been programmed to negate or ignore institutional religion. Indoctrination has definitely occurred. If the generation of descendants of the 50 per cent of post-war children who were sent to Sunday school become more secular – and ongoing secularization surrounds them daily – then it may be that the surviving individual beliefs and spiritualities recede. But not if these spiritualities are meeting an emotional need and are being transmitted within the discourse of the family – those families, that is, in which any discourse occurs. Meanwhile, although their daily lives are secularized, that is to say, operate apparently happily and successfully without reference to institutional religion, many people have religious and spiritual beliefs and values buried in their own minds. These pop out at certain times – bereavement, serious illness, relationship break-ups, even occasionally in casual conversation.

Education is visibly preserving the discourse of religion, but sometimes rather like a fish that has been filleted. God, the backbone of religion, has too often been neatly excised from the presentation. A spineless dead fish on a slab is too often the result. Religious education continues to deal with world religions and the philosophy of religion, in its own way effectively, but it does not address head-on the religious and spiritual situation of Britain. The religious pluralism of British cities has set the agenda for RE, which should be wider. Even the popular post-16 philosophy-of-religion syllabus, in dealing with the traditional proofs of God's existence, ignores why some intelligent people believe now, centuries after these old proofs have been demolished. This syllabus is in that sense an enticing detour from the real task of RE. British religious-education professionals are frequently so concerned to present themselves as non-confessional that they may be transmitting the idea that personal beliefs are somehow an impediment to the job, or that the agnostic teacher does not have the 'baggage' that the religious teacher has in the classroom. This is like the naïve newspaper or internet dating ads that state that prospective partners must have 'no baggage'. The reality is that we all have 'baggage' in emotional, religious and spiritual terms, whether we are believers or atheists.

If education really is preserving the discourse of religion, for the media certainly is not, is religion in safe hands? The answer to this straight question is, as is so often the case with such questions, yes and no. Yes, because a measure of religious knowledge and understanding – much less so in the domain of the spiritual – is being dispensed to the consumers of school education. No, because the education machine itself has no heart and no unifying purpose. Certainly the religious or spiritual development or awareness of children is well down any implicit list of values one can trace from the myriad activities and government publications about education. Yes, because some of the major stakeholders in education are faith communities and in their sectors or ghettos their values are presented, though not always well or, from the point of view of teaching doctrine, successfully. No, because a climate of uncertainty exists around teaching about religion or spirituality that does not extend to the wholesale pumping of secular values into children. This ambiguity towards religion is preserved in the name we take for granted: religious education. We do not talk about teaching history education, or mathematical education. So why religious education? The answer is simple: the British have so many hang-ups about religion that they dare not talk about teaching religion. That would appear highly indoctrinatory and inflammatory. Instead we have the grammatically absurd yet commonplace phrase, teaching religious education. How does one teach education?

Is the UK a special case?

The UK is – once again as in 1940 – one small set of islands against the trend. It is locked in an increasingly secular worldview, yet full of the splendour of heritage religion. It is laced with a pervasive, sur-

viving, immensely diverse spiritual folk religion that relates tangen-
tially to institutional Christianity. It contains smaller institutional
religions coexisting for the most part happily. A struggle for the
mind is undoubtedly in progress, of which many or most individual
minds are quite unaware. Are the British able to appreciate this complex process they are caught up in? How ready are they to face the
issues? Or is the surrender of mind to an uncritical secular worldview inevitable? The British – and to a lesser extent other Europeans
– may be trapped in a secular *Jurassic Park*. The T. Rex of reason has
them in thraldom. Just like the T. Rex of *Jurassic Park* it is not what
it seems.The film's T. Rex was a computer-enhanced model, based
on rubber and wires and pulleys and plastic, a puppet contrivance
and product of the human mind, yet impressive enough to intimidate.
Many people are prisoners of modernity and post-modernity, yet still
cling to spiritualities, some of them pre-modern, even though these
are derided or ignored by many intellectuals. The philosophical critique of modernity and post-modernity, which might liberate these
spiritualities for serious study and at the same time embrace emotional as well as mental intelligence, has not yet reached them.
Beyond our famous 'island fortress' with the electrified perimeter
fences of the mind that our society has erected to imprison our selves
and keep the claims of God and religions outside, there lies a different world. Have we become so institutionalized in this self-con-
structed prison that we cannot bear to leave?

References

1 'Say What You Mean': The Meaning of Indoctrination, Secularization and Education

1 In Snook, I. A. (ed.) (1972), *Concepts of Indoctrination*, London: Routledge & Kegan Paul, pp. 47–8
2 Ziebertz, H. (2003), *Religious Education in a Plural Western Society*, Munster: Lit, p. 12
3 Snook, I. A. (1976), *Indoctrination and Education*, London: Routledge & Kegan Paul, p. 33
4 Ibid., p. 27
5 Ibid., p. 47
6 Barrow, R., and Woods, R. (2nd edn, 1982), *An Introduction to Philosophy of Education*, London: Methuen, p. 67
7 Snook, *Indoctrination and Education*, p. 65
8 Ibid., p. 107
9 In Snook, *Concepts of Indoctrination*, p. 10
10 Ibid., p. 20
11 In Hollins, T. H. B. (ed.) (1964), *Aims in Education*, Manchester: Manchester University Press, p. 35
12 In Spiecker, B., and Straughan, R. (eds) (1991), *Freedom and Indoctrination in Education*, London: Cassell, p. 17
13 In Spiecker, *Freedom and Indoctrination in Education*, pp. 80–1
14 *British Journal of Religious Education*, Vol. 26.1(2004), pp. 10–11
15 Willis Moore in Snook, *Concepts of Indoctrination*, p. 93
16 In Snook, *Concepts of Indoctrination*, p. 128
17 In Spiecker, *Freedom and Indoctrination in Education*, p. 6
18 In Spiecker, *Freedom and Indoctrination in Education*, pp. 37–8
19 In Copley, T., Priestley, J., Coddington, V., Wadman, D. (1991), *Forms of Assessment in Religious Education: The Main Report of the FARE Project*, Exeter: University of Exeter School of Education, 1.1, p. 7
20 Bailey, E. (2001), *The Secular Faith Controversy*, London: Continuum, pp. 54ff.

21 In Höpfl, H. (ed.) (1991), *Luther and Calvin on Secular Authority*, Cambridge: Cambridge University Press, p. 49

22 Chadwick, O. (1975), *The Secularization of the European Mind in the 19th Century*, Cambridge: Cambridge University Press, p. 4

23 Wilson, B. (1976), *Contemporary Transformations of Religion*, Oxford: Oxford University Press, p. 20

24 Ibid., pp. 86, 90

25 Ibid., p. 16

26 Byrne, J. (1996), *Glory, Jest and Riddle: Religious Thought in the Enlightenment*, London: SCM Press, p. 229

27 Mascall, E. L. (1965), *The Secularization of Christianity*, London: Darton, Longman & Todd, p. 190

28 Towler, R., and Coxon, A. P. M. (1979), *The Fate of the Anglican Clergy*, London: Macmillan, p. 142

29 Toynbee, A. (1956), *An Historian's Approach to Religion*, London: Oxford University Press, p. 180

30 In Parsons, G. (ed.) (1993), *The Growth of Religious Diversity: Britain from 1945*, London: Routledge, I, pp. 340–1

31 Hastings, A. (1991), *A History of English Christianity 1920–1990*, London: SCM Press, p. 670

32 Gilbert, A. D. (1980), *The Making of Post-Christian Britain*, London: Longman, p. 17

33 Berger, P. L. (1969), *The Social Reality of Religion*, London: Faber & Faber, p. 134

34 Berger, P. L. (1992), *A Far Glory*, New York: Anchor, pp. 18, 21

35 Berger, *Social Reality of Religion*, p. 111

36 Habgood, J. (1983), *Church and Nation in a Secular Age*, London: Darton, Longman & Todd, p. 50

37 Ibid., p. 22

38 Gilbert, *Making of Post-Christian Britain*, p. 13

39 Chadwick, *Secularization of the European Mind*, p. 258

40 Bailey, *Secular Faith Controversy*, pp. 54ff.

41 Ibid., p. 51

42 Akhtar, S. (1990), *The Light in the Enlightenment: Christianity and the Secular Heritage*, London: Grey Seal, p. 169

43 Thompson, F. (1983 [1939]), *Lark Rise to Candleford*, London: Oxford University Press, pp. 14–15

44 *British Journal of Religious Education*, Vol. 26.1 (2004), p. 8

45   In Sandhurst, B. G. (1946, 2nd edn, 1948), *How Heathen is Britain?*, London: Collins, p. 9
46   Gill, E. (1936), *The Necessity of Belief*, London: Faber & Faber, p. 12
47   Niblett, W. R. (1960), *Christian Education in a Secular Society*, Oxford: Oxford University Press, p. 2

2 The Choking Cradle?: Religion Under Threat in English Society

1   Chadwick, O. (1966), *The Victorian Church* (2 vols), London: A. & C. Black, II, pp. 363–9
2   Ibid., p. 423
3   *Secular Review* (1876 collected volumes), London: National Secular Society, I, 8, p. 21
4   J. Whiteley in *Secular Review*, I, 8, p. 58
5   Byrne, J. (1996), *Glory, Jest and Riddle: Religious Thought in the Enlightenment*, London: SCM Press, p. 31
6   Meyrick, F. (1902), *Sunday Observance*, London: Skeffington & Son, pp. ix, 118
7   Trevelyan, W. B. (1903), *Sunday*, London: Longmans, Green & Co., p. 1
8   Ibid., p. 253
9   Figgis, J. N. (1911), *Religion and English Society*, London: Longmans, Green & Co., p. 19
10   Huxley, T. H. (1909), *Science and Christian Tradition*, London: Macmillan, pp. 238–9
11   Rutherford, M. (1881), *The Autobiography of Mark Rutherford*, London: Hodder & Stoughton; Rutherford, M. (1885), *The Deliverance of Mark Rutherford*, London: Hodder & Stoughton. See also Copley, T. (2000), *Spiritual Development in the State School*, Exeter: University of Exeter Press, pp. 40–6
12   Drummond, A. L. (1950), *The Churches in English Fiction*, Leicester: Edgar Backus, p. xi
13   Copley, *Spiritual Development in the State School*, pp. 46ff.
14   Chadwick, *Victorian Church*, I, p. 425
15   Gay, J. D. (1971), *The Geography of Religion in England*, London: Duckworth, p. 80
16   Chadwick, *Victorian Church*, II, p. 472

17 Chadwick, O. (1975), *The Secularization of the European Mind in the 19th century*, Cambridge: Cambridge University Press, p. 10
18 Figgis, *Religion and English Society*, p. v
19 Ibid., pp. 12–13, 18
20 Ibid., p. 32
21 Ibid., p. 37
22 Wilson, A. N. (1999), *God's Funeral*, London: John Murray, p. 281
23 Sandhurst, B. G. (1946, 2nd edn, 1948), *How Heathen is Britain?*, London: Collins, p. 9
24 Ibid., p. 157
25 J. W. C. Wand in Carpenter, S. C., *et al.* (1947), *Has the Church Failed?*, London: Odhams Press, p. xi
26 In Carpenter, *Has the Church Failed?*, p. 79
27 In Carpenter, *Has the Church Failed?*, p. 82
28 In Carpenter, *Has the Church Failed?*, p. 107
29 Sangster, W. E. (1938), *Methodism Can Be Born Again*, London: Hodder & Stoughton, p. 22
30 Wood, H. G. (1941), *Christianity and Civilisation*, Cambridge: Cambridge University Press, pp. 149ff.
31 Rowntree, R. Seebohm, and Lavers, G. R. (1951), *English Life and Leisure*, London: Longmans, Green & Co.
32 Ibid., p. 361
33 Chadwick, *Secularization of the European Mind*, p. 29
34 Jenkins, D. (2000), *Market Whys and Human Wherefores*, London: Cassell, p. 11
35 Ibid., p. 17
36 Ibid., p. 238
37 Ibid., p. 239
38 In Carpenter, *Has the Church Failed?*, p. 111
39 Chadwick, *Secularization of the European Mind*, p. 179
40 N. Simpson in Arthur, C. (ed.) (1993), *Religion and the Media*, Cardiff: University of Wales Press, p. 10
41 In Arthur, *Religion and the Media*, pp. 14, 173
42 In Arthur, *Religion and the Media*, p. 225
43 In Arthur, *Religion and the Media*, p. 59
44 In Arthur, *Religion and the Media*, p. 92
45 Williams, F., and Gidney, C. (2002); *Vicar to Dad's Army*, Norwich: The Canterbury Press, p. 131

46 Akhtar, S. (1990), *The Light in the Enlightenment: Christianity and the Secular Heritage*, London: Grey Seal, p. x
47 Ibid., p. 7
48 Chadwick, *Secularization of the European Mind*, p. 26
49 Luckman, T. (1967), *The Invisible Religion*, London: Macmillan, pp. 112ff.
50 In Arthur, *Religion and the Media*, p. 56
51 Ibid.

3 'I've Got a Dog Now': The Death and Life of Christianity after 1945

1 In Heelas, P. (1998), *Religion, Modernity and Postmodernity*, Oxford: Blackwell, pp. 218ff.
2 Pratt, V. (1970), *Religion and Secularization*, London: Macmillan, p. 76
3 In Parsons, G. (ed.) (1993), *The Growth of Religious Diversity, Britain from 1945*, London: Routledge, I, p. 314
4 1968 sermon in Jenkins, D. E. (1990), *Still Living with Questions*, London: SCM Press, p. 30
5 Ibid., p. 33
6 Brierley, P. (2000), *The Tide is Running Out*, London: Christian Research, p. 19 and especially p. 23
7 Ibid., p. 129
8 In Obelkervitch, J. and Catterall, P. (eds) (1994), *Understanding Post War British Society*, London: Routledge, p. 174
9 Nigel Pickard, ITV web site, 18 February 2004.
10 Donovan, P. (1997) *All Our Todays: 40 Years of Radio 4's 'Today' Programme*, London: Jonathan Cape, p. 155
11 Ibid., p. 151
12 Prebish, C. S. (1993), *Religion and Sport: The Meeting of Sacred and Profane*, Connecticut: Greenwood Press, pp. 46ff.
13 Ibid., p. 62
14 Niblett, W. R. (1960), *Christian Education in a Secular Society*, Oxford: Oxford University Press, p. 20
15 Greene, G. (1969, 1972 edn), *Travels with my Aunt*, London: The Bodley Head, p. 151
16 Greene, G. (1971), *A Sort of Life*, London: The Bodley Head, p. 165

17 Hornsby-Smith, M. P. (1991), *Roman Catholic Beliefs in England*, Cambridge: Cambridge University Press, p. 214
18 Hinde, R. A. (1999) *Why Gods Persist*, London: Routledge, p. 44
19 In Heron, A. (1999), *Quakers in Britain: A Century of Change 1895–1995*, Kelso: Curlew Graphics, p. 73
20 Britain Yearly Meeting of the Religious Society of Friends (Quakers) (1994), *Quaker Faith and Practice,* London: Britain Yearly Meeting, section 27. 01
21 Heron, *Quakers in Britain*, p. 117
22 Ibid., p. 133
23 Sangster, W. E. (1938), *Methodism Can Be Born Again*, London: Hodder & Stoughton, pp. 70ff.
24 Ibid., pp. 21ff.
25 In Brierley, *Tide is Running Out*, p. 237
26 Bonhoeffer, D. (1971 [1945]), *Letters and Papers From Prison*, London: SCM Press, Letter, 30 April 1944
27 Ibid., Letter, 29 May 1944
28 Ibid., Letter, 8 July 1944
29 Hastings, A. (1991), *A History of English Christianity 1920–1990*, London: SCM Press, p. 34
30 *British Journal of Religious Education*, Vol. 26.1 (2004), p. 17
31 In *Growth of Religious Diversity*, I, p. 341
32 Abercrombie, N., and Warde A. (3rd edn, 2000), *Contemporary British Society*, London: Polity Press, p. 33
33 *The Times*, 10 April 2004
34 Lyon, D. (2000), *Jesus in Disneyland: Religion in Postmodern Times*, Cambridge: Polity Press, p. x
35 Ibid., p. xi
36 Ibid., p. 3
37 Ibid., p. 18
38 Ibid., p. 24
39 Brierley, *Tide is Running Out*, p. 141
40 In Heelas, *Religion, Modernity and Postmodernity*, pp. 72ff.
41 Lyon, *Jesus in Disneyland*, pp. 106ff.
42 Hindmarsh in Lyon, *Jesus in Disneyland*, p. 108
43 Copley, C., *et al.* (2004), *On the Side of the Angels: The Third Report of the Biblos Project*, Exeter: University of Exeter School of Education; Copley, T. (1998), *Echo of Angels: The First Report of the Biblos Project*, Exeter: Exeter University

School of Education; (2001), *Where Angels Fear to Tread: The Second Report of the Biblos Project*, Exeter: University of Exeter School of Education; Copley, T., and Walshe, K. (2002), *The Figure of Jesus in Religious Education*, Exeter: University of Exeter School of Education

44 Such as the Mann-Whitney U Test and LSAS and SDAS attitude tests

45 Norman, E. (2002), *Secularisation*, London: Continuum, p. 12

46 Catholic Education Service 2003 figures

4 Spiritual Fruits, not Religious Nuts: Replacing 'Religion' with 'Spirituality'

1 Nye, R., and Hay, D. (1998), *The Spirit of the Child*, London: Fount, p. 145

2 Booth, C. (1881), *Papers on Godliness*, London: Salvation Army Headquarters, p. 123

3 McPhillips, K., and Mudge, P. *Journal of Religious Education*, 52.1 (2004), p. 10

4 Merton, T. (2003 [1961]), *New Seeds of Contemplation*, Boston, USA: Shambhala, p. 148f.

5 *Western Morning News*, 22 March 2004, p. 2

6 T. Walter in Richards, J., Wilson, S., Woodhead, L. (eds) (1999), *Diana: The Making of a Media Saint*, London: I. B. Tauris, p. 197

7 J. Richards in Richards, Wilson, Woodhead, *Diana: The Making of a Media Saint*, p. 135

8 In Walter, T. (ed.) (1999), *The Mourning for Diana*, Oxford: Berg, p. 37

9 In Walter, *Mourning for Diana*, pp. 145–6

10 Davies, J. (2000), *Diana: A Cultural History*, Basingstoke: Palgrave, p. 183

11 Ibid., p. 187

12 Ibid., p. 137

13 Ibid., p. 126

14 Hinde, R. A. (1999), *Why Gods Persist*, London: Routledge, p. 55

15 Schleiermacher, F. (1958) [1799]: *On Religion Speeches to its Cultured Despisers*, New York: Harper & Bros, 4–5, 39, 71, 276, 282–3

16 Weight, R., and Beach, A. (eds) (1998), *The Right to Belong:*

Citizenship and National Identity in Britain, 1930–1960,
London: I. B. Tauris, p. 22.

17 Weight, R. (2002), *Patriots: National Identity in Britain
1940–2000,* London: Macmillan, p. 11

18 Kumar, K. (2003), *The Making of English National Identity,*
Cambridge: Cambridge University Press, p. 37

19 Weight, *Patriots,* p. 441

20 Kumar, *Making of English National Identity,* pp. 187–8

21 BBC web-site reporting of Radio 4 'Thoughts for the Day', 17
August 2004, <www.bbc.co.uk/manchester/content/articles/
2004/08/17/bishop_hymn_ban_feature>

22 Rasmussen, L. (ed.) (1989), *Reinhold Niebuhr: Theologian of
Public Life,* London: Collins, p. 271

23 Lyon, D. (2000), *Jesus in Disneyland: Religion in Postmodern
Times,* Cambridge: Polity Press, pp. 69–70

5 Education or Catastrophe?

1 Copley, T., Priestley, J., Coddington, V., Wadman, D. (1991),
*Forms of Assessment in Religious Education: The Main Report
of the FARE Project,* Exeter: University of Exeter School of
Education, p. 8

2 Copley, T. (1997), *Teaching Religion: Fifty Years of Religious
Education in England and Wales,* Exeter: University of Exeter
Press, Ch. 1

3 Hansard, 4 August 1943, Column 990

4 Ibid., Columns 1003, 1004

5 Ibid., Column 1020

6 See *The Times* leader by Simon Jenkins, 5 April 2003, 'Who
cares if I drop a surd at 50 paces?'

7 Al-Jallad, M. Z. (1997), 'The Islamic Studies Curriculum in
Jordan', unpublished PhD thesis, University of Manchester

8 Acland, R. (1963), *We Teach Them Wrong,* London: Gollancz;
Goldman, R. (1964), *Religious Thinking from Childhood to
Adolescence,* London: Routledge & Kegan Paul; (1965),
Readiness for Religion, London: Routledge & Kegan Paul;
Loukes, H. (1961), *Teenage Religion,* London: SCM Press

9 Copley, T., in *British Journal of Religious Education,* 20.1
(1998)

10 Grimmitt, M., *What Can I Do in RE?*, Great Wakering: Mayhew-McCrimmon, p. 26
11 E.g. Thompson, P. (2004), *Whatever Happened to Religious Education?*, Cambridge: Lutterworth Press, pp. 7–20
12 Cooling, T., 'Objectivity in Modern Religious Education', *British Journal of Religious Education,* 8.3 (1986)
13 Willey, T. (1982), *Teaching in Multicultural Britain,* York: Longman Resources Unit, pp. 53ff.
14 Lynch, J. (1986), *Multicultural Education: Approaches and Paradigms,* Nottingham: University of Nottingham School of Education, pp. 28ff.
15 *Woman's Own*, 31 October 1987
16 Qualifications and Curriculum Authority web site, <www.qca.org.uk>
17 Walford, R. (2001), *Geography in British Schools, 1850–2000,* London: Woburn Press
18 J. M. Hull in Copley, T., *et al.* (eds) (1997), *Splashes of God-Light*, Swindon: Bible Society, p. 50
19 Copley, T. (1998), *Echo of Angels: The First Report of the Biblos Project*, Exeter: University of Exeter School of Education, p. 16
20 Copley, T., and Copley, G. (1993), *Religious Education in Key Stage 1: A Practical Guide*, Exmouth: Southgate Publishers, pp. 52–4
21 Copley, T., (2000), *Spiritual Development in the State School*, Exeter: University of Exeter Press, pp. 86ff.

6 Fighting a Vapour?: Secularization, Religion, Education and the Future

1 Oldham, J. H. (1931), *Christian Education: Its Meaning and Its Mission*, London: Allen & Unwin, p. 4
2 Gardner, H. (1983, 2nd edn, 1993), *Frames of Mind: The Theory of Multiple Intelligences*, London: Heinemann, p. xxviii
3 Ibid., p. xxix
4 1988 lecture in Jenkins, D. E. (1990), *Still Living with Questions*, London: SCM Press, p. 111
5 *The Big Issue in the North*, No. 505, 23–9 February 2004
6 Bamford, T. W. (ed.) (1970), *Thomas Arnold on Education*, Cambridge: Cambridge University Press, pp. 86ff.

7 For a fuller treatment of Arnold, see Copley, T. (2002), *Black Tom: Arnold of Rugby, the Myth and the Man*, London: Continuum International

8 Merton, T. (2003 [1961]), *New Seeds of Contemplation*, Boston, USA: Shambhala, p. 23

Bibliography and Further Reading

Abercrombie, N., and Warde, A. (3rd edn, 2000), *Contemporary British Society*, London: Polity Press

Acland, R. (1963), *We Teach Them Wrong*, London: Gollancz

Ahern, G., and Davie, G. (1987), *Inner City God*, London: Hodder & Stoughton

Akhtar, S. (1990), *The Light in the Enlightenment: Christianity and the Secular Heritage*, London: Grey Seal

Armstrong, K. (2000), *The Battle for God*, London: HarperCollins

Arthur, C. (ed.) (1993), *Religion and the Media*, Cardiff: University of Wales Press

Bailey, E. (2001), *The Secular Faith Controversy*, London: Continuum

Bamford, T. W. (ed.) (1970), *Thomas Arnold on Education*, Cambridge: Cambridge University Press

Barrow, R., and Woods, R. (2nd edn, 1982), *An Introduction to Philosophy of Education*, London: Methuen

Bernstein, B. (2000), *Pedagogy, Symbolic Control and Identity*, Maryland: Rowman & Littlefield

Brayshaw, A. N. (1921), *The Quakers*, York: William Sessions

Berger, P. L. (1969), *The Social Reality of Religion*, London: Faber & Faber

Berger, P. L. (1992), *A Far Glory*, New York: Anchor

Berger, P. L., 'The Desecularization of the World: A Global Overview', *The National Interest*, 46, Winter 1996/7

Bonhoeffer, D. (1971 [1945]), *Letters and Papers From Prison*, London: SCM Press

Brierley, P. (2000), *The Tide is Running Out*, London: Christian Research

Britain Yearly Meeting of the Religious Society of Friends (Quakers) (1994), *Quaker Faith and Practice*, London: Britain Yearly Meeting

Brown, C. G. (2001), *The Death of Christian Britain*, London: Routledge

Bruce, S. (1995), *Religion in Modern Britain*, Oxford: Oxford University Press

Byrne, J. (1996), *Glory, Jest and Riddle: Religious Thought in the Enlightenment*, London: SCM Press

Carpenter, S. C., *et al.* (1947), *Has the Church Failed?*, London: Odhams Press

Chadwick, O. (1966), *The Victorian Church* (2 vols), London: A. & C. Black

Chadwick, O. (1975), *The Secularization of the European Mind in the 19th Century*, Cambridge: Cambridge University Press

Claussen, D. S. (ed.) (1999), *Sex, Religion, Media*, Maryland: Rowman & Littlefield

Copley, C., *et al.* (2004), *On the Side of the Angels: The Third Report of the Biblos Project*, Exeter: University of Exeter School of Education

Copley, T. (1997), *Teaching Religion: Fifty Years of Religious Education in England and Wales*, Exeter: University of Exeter Press

Copley, T. (1998), *Echo of Angels: The First Report of the Biblos Project*, Exeter: University of Exeter School of Education

Copley, T., 'Re-discovering the Past: Writings on RE in Religion in Education Quarterly, 1934–1939', *British Journal of Religious Education*, 20.1 (1998)

Copley, T. (2000), *Spiritual Development in the State School*, Exeter: University of Exeter Press

Copley, T., 'Teaching the Bible in Religious Education', *Journal of Religious Education*, 48.3 (2000)

Copley, T. (2002), *Black Tom: Arnold of Rugby, the Myth and the Man*, London: Continuum International

Copley, T., and Copley, G. (1993), *Religious Education in Key Stage 1: A Practical Guide*, Exmouth: Southgate Publishers

Copley, T., Priestley, J., Coddington, V., Wadman, D. (1991), *Forms of Assessment in Religious Education: The Main Report of the FARE Project*, Exeter: University of Exeter School of Education

Copley, T., *et al.* (eds) (1997), *Splashes of God-Light*, Swindon: Bible Society

Copley, T. *et al.* (2001), *Where Angels Fear to Tread: The Second Report of the Biblos Project*, Exeter: University of Exeter School of Education

Copley, T., and Walshe, K. (2002), *The Figure of Jesus in Religious Education*, Exeter: University of Exeter School of Education

Davie, G. (1994), *Religion in Britain Since 1945: Believing Without Belonging*, Oxford: Blackwell.

Davie, G. (2000), *Religion in Modern Europe: A Memory Mutates*, Oxford: Oxford University Press

Davie, G. (2002), *Europe: The Exceptional Case*, London: Darton, Longman & Todd

Davies, J. (2000), *Diana: A Cultural History*, Basingstoke: Palgrave

Donovan, P. (1997), *All Our Todays: 40 Years of Radio 4's 'Today' Programme*, London: Jonathan Cape

Drummond, A. L. (1950), *The Churches in English Fiction*, Leicester: Edgar Backus

Figgis, J. N. (1911), *Religion and English Society*, London: Longmans, Green & Co.

Gardner, H. (1983, 2nd edn, 1993), *Frames of Mind: The Theory of Multiple Intelligences*, London: Heinemann

Gay, J. D. (1971), *The Geography of Religion in England*, London: Duckworth

Gibbon, E. (1994 [3 vols 1776–88]), *The History of the Decline and Fall of the Roman Empire*, London: Harmondsworth

Gilbert, A. D. (1980), *The Making of Post-Christian Britain*, London: Longman

Gill, E. (1936), *The Necessity of Belief*, London: Faber & Faber

Goldman, R. (1964), *Religious Thinking from Childhood to Adolescence*, London: Routledge & Kegan Paul

Goldman, R. (1965), *Readiness for Religion*, London: Routledge & Kegan Paul

Greene, G. (1969, 1972 edn), *Travels with my Aunt*, London: The Bodley Head

Greene, G. (1971), *A Sort of Life*, London: The Bodley Head

Grimmitt, M., *What Can I do in RE?*, Great Wakering: Mayhew-McCrimmon

Habgood, J. (1983), *Church and Nation in a Secular Age*, London: Darton, Longman & Todd

Hastings, A. (1991), *A History of English Christianity 1920–1990*, London: SCM Press

Heelas, P. (1998), *Religion, Modernity and Postmodernity*, Oxford: Blackwell

Heron, A. (1999), *Quakers in Britain: A Century of Change 1895–1995*, Kelso: Curlew Graphics

Hinde, R. A. (1999), *Why Gods Persist*, London: Routledge

Hollins, T. H. B. (ed.) (1964), *Aims in Education*, Manchester: Manchester University Press

Höpfl, H. (ed.) (1991), *Luther and Calvin on Secular Authority*, Cambridge: Cambridge University Press

Hornsby-Smith, M. P. (1991), *Roman Catholic Beliefs in England*, Cambridge: Cambridge University Press

Huxley, T. H. (1909), *Science and Christian Tradition*, London: Macmillan

Jackson, R. (2004), *Rethinking Religious Education and Plurality*, London: RoutledgeFalmer

Jenkins, D. (1990), *Still Living with Questions*, London: SCM Press

Jenkins, D. (2000), *Market Whys and Human Wherefores*, London: Cassell

Kay, W. K., and Francis, L. J. (1996), *Drift from the Churches*, Cardiff: University of Wales Press

Kumar, K. (2003), *The Making of English National Identity*, Cambridge: Cambridge University Press

Laqueur, T. W. (1976), *Sunday Schools and Working Class Culture 1780–1850*, Yale: Yale University Press

Loukes, H. (1961), *Teenage Religion*, London: SCM Press

Luckman, T. (1967), *The Invisible Religion*, London: Macmillan

Lynch, J. (1986), *Multicultural Education: Approaches and Paradigms*, Nottingham: University of Nottingham School of Education

Lyon, D. (2000), *Jesus in Disneyland: Religion in Postmodern Times*, Cambridge: Polity Press

Martin, D. (1967), *A Sociology of English Religion*, London: Heinemann Educational

Mascall, E. L. (1965), *The Secularization of Christianity*, London: Darton, Longman & Todd

Masters, P., and Watts, M. H. (2000), *The Necessity of Sunday Schools in this Post-Christian Era*, London: Wakeman Trust

Meek, D. E. (2000), *The Quest for Celtic Christianity*, Edinburgh: Handsel Press

Merton, T. (2003 [1961]), *New Seeds of Contemplation*, Boston, USA: Shambhala

Meyrick, F. (1902), *Sunday Observance*, London: Skeffington & Son

Moynihan, B. (2002), *If God Spare My Life: William Tyndale, the English Bible and Sir Thomas More*, London: Little, Brown

Newbigin, L., Sanneh, L., Taylor, J. (1998), *Faith and Power: Christianity and Islam in 'Secular' Britain*, London: SPCK

Niblett, W. R. (1960), *Christian Education in a Secular Society*, Oxford: Oxford University Press

Norman, E. (2002), *Secularisation*, London: Continuum

Nye, R., and Hay, D. (1998), *The Spirit of the Child*, London: Fount

Obelkervitch, J., and Catterall, P. (eds) (1994), *Understanding Post War British Society*, London: Routledge

Oldham, J. H. (1931), *Christian Education: Its Meaning and Its Mission*, London: Allen & Unwin

Osmond, R. (1993), *Changing Christian Culture and Morals in England Today*, London: Darton, Longman & Todd

Parsons, G. (ed.) (1993), *The Growth of Religious Diversity: Britain from 1945*, London: Routledge

Peters, R. S. (1966), *Ethics and Education*, London: Allen & Unwin

Pratt, V. (1970), *Religion and Secularisation*, London: Macmillan

Prebish, C. S. (1993), *Religion and Sport: The Meeting of Sacred and Profane*, Connecticut: Greenwood Press

Qualifications and Curriculum Authority (2001), *Citizenship: Scheme of Work for Key Stage 3*, London: Qualifications and Curriculum Authority

Rasmussen, L. (ed.) (1989), *Reinhold Niebuhr: Theologian of Public Life*, London: Collins

Richards, J., Wilson, S., Woodhead, L. (eds) (1999), *Diana: The Making of a Media Saint*, London: I. B. Tauris

Rowntree, R. Seebohm, and Lavers, G. R. (1951), *English Life and Leisure*, London: Longmans, Green & Co.

Rutherford, M. (1881), *The Autobiography of Mark Rutherford*, London: Hodder & Stoughton

Rutherford, M. (1885), *The Deliverance of Mark Rutherford*, London: Hodder & Stoughton

Ryder, J., and Silver, H. (1970, 3rd edn, 1985), *Modern English Society*, London: Methuen

Sandhurst, B. G. (1946, 2nd edn, 1948), *How Heathen is Britain?*, London: Collins

Sangster, W. E. (1938), *Methodism Can Be Born Again*, London: Hodder & Stoughton

Secular Review (1876 collected volumes), London: National Secular Society

Schleiermacher, F. (1958 [1799]), *On Religion: Speeches to its Cultured Despisers*, New York: Harper & Bros

Smart, N. (1968), *Secular Education and the Logic of Religion*, London: Faber & Faber

Smart, N. (1993), *The Phenomenon of Religion*, London: Macmillan

Smith, R. G. (1966), *Secular Christianity*, London: Collins

Snook, I. A. (1976), *Indoctrination and Education*, London: Routledge & Kegan Paul

Snook, I. A. (ed.) (1972), *Concepts of Indoctrination*, London: Routledge & Kegan Paul

Spiecker, B., and Straughan, R. (eds) (1991), *Freedom and Indoctrination in Education*, London: Cassell

Stangor, C. (ed.) (2000), *Stereotypes and Prejudice*, Philadelphia: Psychology Press

Stout, D. A., and Buddenbaum, J. M. (eds) (1996), *Religion and Mass Media*, London: Sage

Stowe, H. B. (1961 [1852]), *Uncle Tom's Cabin*, London: Dent

Thomas, T. (ed.) (1988), *The British: Their Religious Beliefs and Practices 1800–1986*, London: Routledge

Thompson, F. (1983 [1939]), *Lark Rise to Candleford*, London: Oxford University Press

Thompson, P. (2004), *Whatever Happened to Religious Education?* Cambridge: Lutterworth Press

Towler, R., and Coxon, A. P. M. (1979), *The Fate of the Anglican Clergy*, London: Macmillan

Toynbee, A. (1956), *An Historian's Approach to Religion*, London: Oxford University Press

Trevelyan, W. B. (1903), *Sunday*, London: Longmans, Green & Co.

Walford, R. (2001), *Geography in British Schools*, 1850–2000, London: Woburn Press

Walter, T. (ed.) (1999), *The Mourning for Diana*, Oxford: Berg

Ward, Mrs H. (1888), *Robert Elsmere*, London: Smith Elder

Weight, R. (2002), *Patriots: National Identity in Britain 1940–2000*, London: Macmillan

Weight, R., and Beach A. (eds) (1998), *The Right to Belong:*

Citizenship and National Identity in Britain, 1930–1960, London: I. B. Tauris

Wesleyan Reform Union (2003), *Year Book 2003–04*, Sheffield: Wesleyan Reform Church House

Willey, T. (1982), *Teaching in Multicultural Britain,* York: Longman Resources Unit

Williams, F., and Gidney, C. (2002), *Vicar to Dad's Army*, Norwich: The Canterbury Press

Wilson, A. N. (1999), *God's Funeral*, London: John Murray

Wilson, B. (1976), *Contemporary Transformations of Religion*, Oxford: Oxford University Press

Wood, H. G. (1941), *Christianity and Civilisation*, Cambridge: Cambridge University Press

Ziebertz, H. (2003), *Religious Education in a Plural Western Society*, Munster: Lit

Index

Aktar, S. 11
All Hallows Eve *see* Hallowe'en
Alpha courses 68
*Amazing Technicolor
Dreamcoat, the 1*23
Andrews, W. L. 28 31
Arnold, Matthew ix, 68
Arnold, Thomas 118, 145f.
Ashimolowo, M. 68
Assemblies (in schools) *see*
collective worship
Auschwitz xii, 108
Austen, J. 65
Avalon 90
Aztecs xii

Baha'i 19
Bailey, J. 7, 11
Baptists 68f.
Barclay, R. 58
Bauman, Z. 69
Berger, P. L. 9f.
Biblos Project 45, 73f., 126
Birmingham RE agreed
syllabus, 1975 113, 127
Blake, W. 100
Bonhoeffer, D. 2, 8, 64
Booth, C. 86
Bradlaugh, C. 25, 34
Brainwashing 4
Brierley, P. 68
Britain *see* UK

British Humanist Association
34f., 129
Brown, C. xiv, 46, 65
Buddha, the 92
Buddhism, Buddhists xi 45, 66,
85, 94, 103
Bultmann, R. 2
Bunting, J. 70
Butler, R. A. 107, 128
Byre, J. 8

Campbell, R. 31
Carlyle, T. 23
Carroll, L. 1
Catholic *see* Roman Catholic
Cavell, E. 98
Census on religion 1851 21f.
Census on religion 2001 xiv, 46,
66f., 110, 136
Chadwick, O. 7, 11, 23, 25, 31,
38
Chandler, P. 90
Channel Islands 135
Chesterton, F. 41
China 6
Christmas xvi, 40–3, 148
Church schools ix, 34f., 78ff.
Cinema depictions of religion
37f.
Citizenship 117f.
Clergy xiv, 32f., 36
Collective worship 35, 128–32

Complementary medicine 91
Consumerism 29
Conway, M. 24, 63
Cooling, T. 115
Copley, C. vi, 76–8
Culture, roots of 43f., 145–7
Cupitt, D. 2, 10, 45f.
Curriculum xvif., 106, 111, 133

Darwin, C. 22f.
David and Goliath narrative in
    RE 124–6
Davie, Grace xiv, 48
Dawkins, R. 34
Degree studies *see* Graduateness
Descartes, R. 8
Diana, Princess 89–91, 132
Dickens, C. 24, 40
Disneyland 67
Disraeli, B. 24
Divali 42
Drummond, A. L. 24
Dunblane primary school 89

Ecumenical movement viii
Education Act 1944 xiii, 107f.
Education Reform Act 1988
    111, 128, 130
Education, meanings of term
    13–18
Eid 42
Eliot, G. 23, 36
Empire, British ix, 131
England ix, xiv, xvii, 27, 86, 90
English Church Attendance
    survey (1998) 47f.
European religious identity xvii,
    1f., 6, 25, 28, 45, 66, 68, 83,
    85, 103f., 137, 150

Everett, J. 70
Exeter, University of vi, 7, 73

FARE project 6
Fatalism 93
Father Christmas 40f.
Fell, M. 58
Feuerbach, L. 2
Figgis, J. N. 23, 25f.
Fly Sheets 70
Fore, W. 32
Fox, G. 58f., 63
France 42
Free market, the 30f.
Friend, The 59
Fundamentalism 69, 94, 102,
    115

Gardner, H. 143
Gay, J. 25
Geography teaching 119
Gibbon, E. 23
Gilbert, A. D. 8–10,
    Glastonbury 90, 94–6, 138
Goldman, R. 119
Graduateness 17f.
Gray, T. 78
Greene, G. 56
Grimmitt, M. 114
Guardian, The vi, 32f.
Gurney, J. J. 59
Guru Nanak 42 87

Habgood, J. 10f.
Hallowe'en 39f.
Hardy, T. 23
Hastings, A. 9, 65
Heroes 100, 131f.
Hillsborough football tragedy 88

Hinduism, Hindus 19, 66, 87, 94, 113f., 120
History teaching 5, 149
Hobby, religion as 2
Holy Grail 95
Holyoake, G. J. 22
Hoover, J. E. 101
Hornsby-Smith, M. P. 57
Horoscopy 92
Hot cross buns xvi, 54
Hull, J. 4, 15, 122
Hume, D. 23
Huxley, T. 23

Identity, national ix, xvii, 91, 95, 97–103, 131f., 135f., 139, 149f.
India xiii, 32
Indoctrination, meaning of 2–6
Indoor living, effect of 12f.
Inge, W. R. 62
Islam, Muslims vii, xv, 19, 41f., 66, 80, 82, 96, 111f., 113, 121, 127, 131, 141–4
Islamic education 112
Isle of Man 135

Jainism 19
Jarvis, A. R. 39
Jehovah's Witnesses 60, 115
Jenkins, D. 30f., 46
Jordan 112
Joseph narrative in RE 121–4
Joseph of Arimathea 95
Judaism, Jews 19, 66, 94, 120f., 131, 136f., 141, 144
Jynx 91

Kazepides, T. 6
Kennedy, L. 34
Kilpatrick, W. H. 3
Kingsley, C. 24
Korea *see* North or South Korea

Lady Luck 91
Lambeth Quadrilateral, The 24
Lewis, C. S. 15, 27
Lisbon earthquake (1755) 33
Luckman, T. 38
Lyon, D. 67f.

Mann, H. 21f.
Mascall, E. L. 8
Masters, P. 53
Maths teaching 112, 149
McDonnell, J. 32
Media and religion 31–7, 89f.
Media viii
Medicine *see* complementary medicine
Merton, T. 147
Methodism viii 47f., 63f., 70–2, 115
Meyrick, F. 23
More, H. 50
Morris, C. 32
Mothering Sunday/ Mothers' Day 39
Muhammad 127, 142
Multiculturalism 110f., 115f.
Murray, J. M. 28
Muslims *see* Islam

National Secular Society 6, 34f.
Nayler, J. 58
Nazi Germany xi
New Age 96

New Churches 68f.
New Zealand 5, 74
Niblett, R. 15
Niebuhr, R. 101
Nixon, R. 101
Norman, Edward xiv, 76
North Korea xi, 6
Northern Ireland 101, 135f.

Oelkers, J. 4
Ofsted 16, 119
Orwell, George xi
Osmond, R. 57
Oz, Wizard of 30, 132

Patriotism 98, 102
Penn, W. 58, 60
Personal and social education
    116f.
Peters, R. S. 15
Phillipines xiii
Pinter, H. 34
Potter, B. 23
Pratt, V. 45
Prebish, C. S. 49
Premier Media Group 69
Priestley, J. 108
Propaganda 3
Protestantism 9f., 46, 97f., 144
Protestantism, Liberal 10, 57ff.,
    61, 72, 110, 114
Providence 30

Quakers *see* Religious Society
    of Friends

Raikes, R. 50
Rationalist Press Association 35
RE *see* Religious Education

Religion, meaning of term
    18–20, 83f., 86f., 93f., 144f.
Religious Education xvi, 35, 55,
    80f., 108f., 111–28, 138f.,
    148f.
Religious Society of Friends
    (Quakers) 57–63, 69, 131
Revivalism 72ff., 142f.
Rhodes, C. 100
Roman Catholic Church,
    Catholics vi, xiv, 33, 36, 47f.,
    56f., 80, 131
Rowntree, J. W. 59
Rowntree-Lavers survey 28f.
Rutherford, M. 24

Salvation Army xiii, 86
Sandhurst, B. G. 27
Sangster, W. E. 28, 63, 135
Schleiermacher, F. 93
Schleifer, S. A. 31f.
Scotland xvii, 101, 135f.
Secular Review, The 22f.
Secularists ix, 137f.
Secularization viii, xv, 2,
    process of 7–12, 38–44,
    125f.,141f., 148
September 11th 2001 ('9/11')
    xii, 1, 33
Shopping 10, 12, 29, 40f.
Siegel, H. 6
Sikhism, Sikhs 66, 113, 120, 143
Sisyphus 45
Smart, N. 113
Smith, A. 30
Snook I. A. 3f.
Sölle, D. 32
Songs of Praise 47f.
South Korea xiii

South Place Ethical Society 24
Spiecker, B. 4,
Sport and religion 49f.
Spring-Rice, C. 99
Spurgeon, C. H. 53
Standing Advisory Councils on
    RE, (SACRE) 35
Stephen, Feast of 40
Stephen, L. 23
Stowe, Harriet Beecher xii
Strauss, D. F. 2, 10
Sunday Schools viii, 50–3, 79,
    148
Supermarket xvi,11, 29
Superstition 91
Swann report 115
Syria xiii
Szagun, A. 50

Television 31ff., 49f., 74,
    136
Temple, W. 108ff.
Thompson, F. 12
Thompson, P. 27
Thought for the Day 49, 130f.
Topsy xii
Toronto Blessing 72f.
Toynbee, A. 9, 64
Toynbee, P. 34
Trevelyan, W. B. 23
Tudur, Huw vi, 97
TV *see* television
Tyndale, W. 97

UK ix, xiv, xvii, 8, 36, 91,
    97–103, 115, 131f., 135f.,
    139, 142, 149f.
Unitarians 62

United Reformed Church viii,
    47
USA xiii, xv, 5, 36, 39, 42, 49,
    52, 69, 99, 140

Victorian religious practice 22,
    29

Wales, Welsh culture xii, xvii,
    97f., 101, 135f.
Walley, J. 90
Ward, M. (Mrs Humphry Ward)
    24
Wells, H. G. 105
Wesleyan Methodists *see*
    Methodism
Wesleyan Reform Union vi,
    70–72
Weston-super-Mare ix
White, J. P. 5
White, W. H. *see* Rutherford, M.
Whitehouse, M. 56
Whiting, R. 95
Williams, F. 36
Wilson, A. N. 26
Withdrawal clause in RE 118
Wolffe, J. 9
Women priests *see* clergy
Wood, H. G. 28
Woodruff, D. 28
Worship in schools *see*
    collective worship

Yusuf *see* Joseph

Zambia xiii
Ziebertz, H. 3
Zoroastrianism 19, 140